TREVOR FORD
THE AUTHORISED BIOGRAPHY

TREVOR FORD

THE AUTHORISED BIOGRAPHY

Neil Palmer

Foreword by John Hartson

AMBERLEY

This book is dedicated to my mother, Maria. Her strength, bravery and determination have been an inspiration to me.

First published 2016

Amberley Publishing
The Hill, Stroud
Gloucestershire, GL5 4EP

www.amberley-books.com

Copyright © Neil Palmer, 2016

The right of Neil Palmer to be identified as the Author
of this work has been asserted in accordance with the
Copyrights, Designs and Patents Act 1988.

British Library Cataloguing in Publication Data.
A catalogue record for this book is available from the British Library.

ISBN 978 1 4456 4056 3 (print)
ISBN 978 1 4456 4089 1 (ebook)

Typesetting and Origination by Amberley Publishing.
Printed in the UK.

Contents

Foreword

I was deeply touched and honoured when Neil Palmer contacted me asking if I would write the foreword for a book about Welsh footballing legend Trevor Ford. Although we came from different eras in the game, what connects us is not only our Swansea roots but that we were both proud Welshman who got to wear that coveted number nine shirt for our country. Growing up, my father told me many stories about Trevor and his prowess as a centre forward. He played the game like myself, always giving 100 per cent and never being afraid to shirk a challenge irrespective of the opponent's reputation. This was always my mantra from the very first time I put on a pair of football boots, and as I progressed in the game comparisons to Trevor that were thrown my way gave me the confidence to strive to be better. Trevor was a player who would fight tooth and nail with his opponent for ninety minutes and then shake his hand at the end of the game. Like many of his generation he played the game with pride, honour and respect for his fellow players (even goalkeepers), something that sadly seems to be lacking in today's modern game.

I first met Trevor at an awards ceremony held by the Welsh Football Association; I had picked up an award that evening and then somebody asked me if I would like to meet Trevor Ford. I was taken to his table and we shook hands. He told me loved the way I played the game, and I don't think I have ever met a more humble, dignified man in my life. It was a pleasure to be in his company; within minutes we were just two Swansea boys from different eras talking about the game.

It is fitting that a book should be written about such a character as Trevor. He scored goals wherever he went, even in Holland when he played for PSV Eindhoven, and his performances in the Welsh red shirt are legendary. Who knows what would have happened if he had gone to the World Cup in Sweden in 1958. What we do know is off the pitch his stand against directors of clubs and those who governed football helped change the game for every pro today. He was a credit to the number nine shirt and a credit to the game he helped change. It is a privilege to be part of a story about one of Wales' greats.

John Hartson

Acknowledgements

Writing a book can be a very isolating experience; the old phrase 'an appointment with self-doubt' seems quite fitting as that's exactly what it is you encounter as you sit in front of a blank computer screen wondering if the original idea that brought you here in the first place will be good enough to fill the page. It's moments like this when you need those around you; therefore I would like to thank my wife, Sally, for her continued support and incredible belief in every project I have ever undertaken. I want to also thank my children, Sophie and Jack, as well as my parents, Maria and Glyn, for their interest in this book. Thanks also must go to my in-laws, Roger and Pauline, who again have shown real interest in this book from its early stages. The encouragement of these people has gotten me through on occasions.

Its great having an idea but you need also a team to put things in place practically and this book would certainly not have happened without the honest and passionate encouragement of David Ford – I hope we will always be friends. Thanks must also go to the people whose thoughts and memories fill this book – again without them I would have nothing to write – so a very big thank you, in no particular order, to Ceri Stennett, John Hartson, Gordon Taylor, Billy Bingham, Stan Anderson, Simon Goodyear, Thommy Thompson, Rob Mason, Mel Charles, Colin Baker, Alan Harrington, Andy Malloy, Alan Curtis, Terry Medwin, Cliff Jones, Andrew Taylor, Frans Claes, Annette Rodrick. I have to admit that is quite a formidable team; thank you guys, I will be forever in your debt. Also I would like to thank all the staff at

Amberley Publishing for getting this book off the ground – thank you for believing in the idea from the start. Finally, a big thank you must go to all those people who responded after I put out a plea for memories of Trevor Ford. There has been a certain weight of responsibility in the writing of this book, as Trevor was so well loved, so I hope I have done all of you proud.

Introduction

It was a March evening in Cardiff City's 1992/93 season, a season in which the Bluebirds won promotion out of football's bottom tier and also added a Welsh Cup under the excellent stewardship of manager Eddie May, when I sat in the grandstand at Ninian Park with my father to watch the game against Scarborough (yes, following football is not all glamour). The game will always stay in my mind, not for the 1-0 win by the Bluebirds but because at around ten minutes after kick-off my Dad nudged me and pointed out that a couple of rows away, sat next to the aisle, was Trevor Ford. When he told me, the game suddenly lost a lot of its interest: I would glance at the match while keeping an eye on this grey-haired gentleman in a light-brown overcoat constantly being asked for his autograph by a whole array of supporters. My mind drifted back to my childhood, as the name Trevor Ford will always be synonymous with how my father judged any centre forward of worth during the 1960s through to today – Dad tended to do this with singers, saying such things as 'They're not as good as Sinatra.' Well for him no centre forward was 'as good as Trevor Ford'. The comparison was a little lost on me as I was brought up in the football sticker and Esso coin era of the players of the 1960s and 1970s, and to be honest my only knowledge, apart from my father's cast-iron opinion of him being the best, was of a photograph of him in an old Charles Buchan football book that showed Trevor in an Aston Villa kit, something that fascinated me as the shirt had a laced-up neck. However, I watched Ford throughout the game, and when it ended my father and I made our way out of the stand, which just happened to mean passing Trevor Ford. As we did my father said 'hello Trevor' and offered his hand, which Trevor then shook. Although I was in my thirties I felt like a child, rooted to the spot on meeting a famous person, and I just nodded in return of Trevor's smile. All the way home we talked about his career. My Dad explained how he was the big star at Cardiff City when he was part of the ground staff, all of which I had heard many times from Dad, but to see the man in the flesh seemed to give these stories even more merit.

Trevor was a player that stayed in my subconscious. When I started writing sports books I had the honour of interviewing various football players from the 1950s and I would always ask them, for my own curiosity more than anything else, what was Trevor Ford like? Man to man they would always talk affectionately about him, yet anytime he was mentioned in the media he was always referred to as 'Fiery Ford' or 'Terrible Trevor', which I thought was a little unjust. Even when he passed away the main bulk of any obituary in the newspapers tended to be based largely on his book *I Lead the Attack* and didn't much include the prolific goal stats for his clubs and Wales. And with the upsurge in Welsh football I started to think he was forgotten about by sections of the media as they talked about 'greats' like John Charles, Ian Rush, Ryan Giggs, Ivor Allchurch and Gareth Bale, all of whom are quite rightly great Welsh footballers, but I always felt there was room for one more. Unfortunately this was the same when pundits talked about great centre forwards. It appeared that the modern generation of media, with its seven-days-a-week football, internet forums and radio talk shows, only went as far back as Gary Lineker and Italia 90. I make no apologies for my continued frustration at this, even at the cost of being called a grumpy old git – it is a title that when it comes to the recognition of 'old' footballers, I wear with pride.

So with this in mind, I started on path of finding out about Trevor Ford in detail with a view for a book .The writer L. P. Hartley memorably began his novel *The Go Between* with the words 'The past is a foreign country: they do things differently there.' And that has never been truer when you look at the football world in the 1950s, which has now become unrecognisable today. Trevor was at the very centre of the struggle for players to earn a better deal out of the game; it has been said many times that he was a player who knew his own worth. He knew early on, even in his Swansea Town days, that he was the main attraction when it came to putting bums on seats, and football club directors knew it. Why else would they purchase the very best players to enhance their football clubs; after all, nobody said 'I can't wait for Saturday to see the left-back play.' Trevor knew that as a centre forward he had a certain cache that clubs would pay for. The problem was that in the eyes of the football authorities everybody got their £20 a week, and that was their lot. In truth this was never going to work – nor did it. It insults our intelligence to think that a young seventeen-year-old at Wolverhampton Wanderers would be paid the same £20 per week that Wolves and England captain Billy Wright would get, or that another seventeen-year-old at Preston North End would get the same as Legend Tom Finney. The answer is obviously no. The reality was that your Billy Wrights and Tom Finneys were, like every other top player, given various gifts that would make their stay at a club more comfortable. The players knew what was going on and so did the directors, but it took strong individuals like Trevor to stand up for change in the game. This resulted in a stronger PFA who were able to negotiate an end to the maximum wage and the ability for players to be in control of their own contracts. Trevor's subsequent confrontations with authorities tarnished him with the tag of being trouble, and not one to touch in terms of bringing to a club, yet his goal-scoring record sits alongside many of the greats in the game, past or present. The most damming part of his career was his treatment by the Welsh FA when they did not take him to Sweden as part of the Welsh 1958 World Cup squad, a decision that saw many Welsh selectors flex their muscles towards Trevor, making sure they taught him a lesson for what they deemed as embarrassing the organisation rather than doing what was the best thing for the country. As it turned out, the lack of preparation and the amateurish attitude of the Welsh FA in the finals reconfirmed that many of the so-called 'selectors' should never have been within 100 yards of running a football team in the first place.

During the research for this book I was honoured to meet Trevor's son David, who gave his support to the project. David's honesty and enthusiasm to tell his father's story, warts and all, has been a real driving force of the book; he has allowed me to share with you, the reader, everything about his father and the Ford family. David allowed me the chance to experience Trevor the man, and numerous ex-colleagues allowed me the chance to experience Trevor the player. I will always be thankful to them for that.

1

Humble Beginnings

When Trevor and Daisy Ford's second son Trevor arrived into the world on 1 October 1923, they could not have dreamt of the legacy this young lad from Townhill, Swansea, would have on his chosen sport of football. Young Trevor was born into a world that had just come out of the First World War, and as countries recovered from the hardships that had been enforced by the conflict, it instilled a new kind of attitude in many people. Many had seen the horrors of the war; young lads had spent terrible times in trenches and women had kept industry alive back home and raised families on their own. Times were tough, yet it led to a realisation of how short life could be, and this attitude seemed to be getting Britain back on its feet. With a need for coal, copper and steel manufacturing, Trevor's home town of Swansea would be one of the benefactors of a new dock built for the increased industry, as well as housing for many of the new workers. Unfortunately, by the end of the decade the Great Depression would set in. Triggered by the Wall Street Crash in New York, the UK government, like those in many European countries, was still struggling with the massive debts they had incurred during the First World War, and therefore events in New York had served to intensify the financial crisis. Grinding economies to a halt, these events would rip the very heart out of Britain and Wales – 1927 would see 23 per cent of the Welsh workforce unemployed, something that Wales as a nation would forever struggle to recover from. All of these factors meant things would be very tough for any couple bringing up children in that time, and the Ford family in Swansea were no exception. Trevor and Daisy lived at Merlin Crescent in the Townhill area; it was a large council site that had its roots firmly entrenched in the Labour movement. A working-class area that sat high above the town of Swansea, most of the houses were three-bedroom and semi-detached with outdoor toilets and a small patch of garden. Compared to the smaller terraced cottages in the town, this new estate was the height of luxury. Trevor was a PT instructor during the First World War and was a keen sportsman – he once harboured dreams of being a professional in football or cricket – but like so many gifted amateurs at that time, the war put an end to such dreams. Sport was very important to Trevor and he would encourage his three sons, Ivor, Trevor Jnr and Ronald, to enjoy it whenever they could, although it seemed that only young Trevor Jnr would inherit his father's love of sport. Daisy stayed at home like most women on the estate at the time; she cooked and cleaned for the family, which also included the couple's youngest child, daughter Joan. The Townhill estate was a very close-knit community – the women looked after each other's children – and although food was scarce at times, the kids always seemed to be able to get a meal from home or a neighbour.

Returning from the First World War with no qualified trade, Trevor first gained employment as a van driver in the Swansea area. It was a job he loved due to the variation of each day and was a change from the town's main industries, the coal mines and steelworks, work he would freely admit was backbreaking for any man. Unfortunately Trevor Snr was made redundant by his delivery firm, and after weeks of hardship for the family he gained a job at the local Tower cinema on the estate. The Towerhill cinema was a large Victorian building with beautiful ornate ceilings and expensive fittings. From the inside it gave the feeling of grandeur and opulence, quite a contrast to when the customers exited through the grand double doors and returned to their tough hard working lives, having just spent a couple of hours lost in the latest blockbuster films of the day, such as *The Hunchback of Notre Dame*, starring Lon Cheyney, or *The Love Nest*, starring Buster Keaton. During his time at the cinema, Trevor rose to the position of manager and was able to treat Daisy to nights at the cinema once in a while, along with making his children very popular with their peers by turning a blind eye to payment if they arrived at the cinema with friends to see the latest cartoons. Although money was tight for the couple, Trevor's love of sport, and young Trevor's growing ability in football, meant that he always found the money for his son to have a new pair of boots every birthday. Speaking in his excellent autobiography of 1957, *I Lead the Attack*, Trevor recalls his father's support towards his fledgling career:

> Each time my birthday came around he would hand me my present – a pair of football boots and a ball. The gift never varied, true, the boots got bigger year by year and the ball went up a couple of sizes. Often when I got home from Powys Avenue School he would be standing at the garden gate waiting for me with my football boots over his shoulder and my ball tucked under his arm. 'C'mon son' he would say. 'Let's nip down Paradise Park for a kick around.'

Trevor and his father would spend many evenings playing together in the park at the end of the road, and Trevor would spend hours teaching the young Trevor techniques on how to make him a better player. The two of them would come home filthy as they both battled to win the ball, but Trevor knew that if his young son could improve his skills he had a better chance of one day making it as a professional. Though it could be perceived that Trevor was a 'pushy parent', the reality was he recognised his son's talent and knowing how hard times had been, he just wanted to give him the best sporting start possible and spare him the gruelling future that the pit or the steelworks offered him. One day Trevor spotted that young Trevor's left foot was weaker than his right, so he met him in the park with a boot and a plimsoll. Trevor put the plimsoll on his son's strong right foot and the boot on the weaker left. They played for hours while all the time making Trevor's left foot stronger and as good as the right.

Due to Trevor Snr's job, which meant he was always working Saturdays, he rarely got the chance to go down to the Vetch field with his boys and see Swansea Town play, although this never stopped Trevor and his mates. They would regularly climb up onto a garden wall to see stars such as Jack Fowler and Joe Sykes before trying to emulate them in the playground on Monday. At the time Swansea Town were in the Second Division of the football league, and those men in white shirts were real heroes to Trevor and his mates. It was at the Powys Avenue School where Trevor really began to show his talent as a footballer. Local historian Annette Rodrick remembers the school vividly:

> It was a large wooden single story building, a mixed school with about 30 children per class aged between 7 and 11. It served the local community well; I remember we couldn't go when we had snowfall, as there wasn't any heating due to the pipes freezing! They had outside toilets where the ice used to freeze in the toilet pan and sometimes crack the pan, which was a bit dangerous if you were sat on it, I also remember the cut up squares of newspaper hanging on a hook as toilet paper. The playground was a mix of ash and grit so we were always falling down and getting cuts and bruises. At the end of the playground was Paradise Park and this is where the boys would play football or rugby or cricket in the summer. The park was really the centre for all the local children's games.

Trevor became captain of the school team, playing centre-half even though he was a lot smaller than some of the other lads in the side; it was his ability and determination that shone through even at that young age. When Trevor was eleven he left Powys Avenue School for the adjoining senior school Townhill; the school was a large imposing Victorian building that had boys and girls segregated. The boys played football or rugby in the winter and cricket in the summer; the girls played shinty – a form of hockey that some would say was more violent than rugby. Ernie Windsor, who was two years younger than Trevor and is now well into his eighties, remembers Trevor at that time:

> I used to live on the Townhill road which was at the end of Trevor's road at Merlins Crescent. He was always the best sportsman in the area, if we were picking teams whether it be cricket in the summer, or the usual 25-a-side football match we would often play, everybody wanted Trevor in the team. You could never get the ball from him, he was really strong and tough both on and

off the pitch; you wouldn't have messed with him as he could certainly handle himself even as a 13-year-old. I once saw him have a fight on the corner of Merlin Crescent because some lad said his dad's cinema was rubbish, I can understand how all those goalkeepers' years later were so scared of him. He was no bully though, he just got on with things and had a laugh and a joke. When I joined Powys Avenue School Trevor was already there as he was older than me and he was very popular with everyone, especially the girls, but even then he was only ever really interested being a footballer. He knew he was better than everybody else but he wasn't big-headed about it, like some kids would have been. That's why we were all so pleased when he made it.

At Townhill, Trevor came under the influence of sports teacher David Benyon, who also happened to run the Swansea Boys team. Benyon made a tremendous impact over the years on Swansea schoolboy football. He believed that football was character-forming and that you had to have principles on and off the pitch. Many of the town's great players came under his guidance over the years. Benyon treated youngsters as mature and responsible young men, an attitude that struck a chord with young Trevor. Again speaking in his autobiography, Trevor recalls David Benyon with affection:

He had the patience of a saint; he was modest and had a deep understanding and knowledge of football. It was his great love in life to pass it on to the youngsters. Nothing was too much trouble for him; he gave up three nights a week for our benefit and was always available if we needed his advice on a fourth night. He would say 'Listen here Trevor, let the ball do the work for you. Look at those lads over there, see what they're doing? They all want to be where the ball is. See how they are running all over the park? And here's one chap, who now he's got the ball wants to keep it, unlike the chap over there who just wants to belt it up field. That's all wrong. You must hold your position and work as a member of a team, thinking at all times of distribution.'

Wise words indeed from Mr Benyon; in fact, it is a philosophy that is still relevant to schoolboy football today more than eighty years later. Trevor excelled in Benyon's Swansea boys team, playing as full-back and getting the interest of not only his local side but also the Welsh selectors. Just after his thirteenth birthday, Trevor was called to Mr Benyon's class. Fearing he had done something wrong, Benyon informed the youngster that he had been selected to play for Wales at Under-14 level, in a series of matches against the other home nations. Trevor raced home and ran into the arms of his bewildered father, and was so excited he could barely get his words out as he attempted to tell them of his wonderful news. The whole family were ecstatic and neighbours called in to wish their new star good luck, but unfortunately days before Trevor's debut against Scotland he broke his ankle in a tackle playing for the school team. Trevor was inconsolable and cried himself to sleep; without doubt his father and the rest of the family were doing the same in the next room. However, his father masked his obvious disappointment with encouragement towards his heartbroken son, telling him that he would still play for Wales one day. All was not lost, and after weeks in plaster Trevor's ankle healed and he was soon back to playing football and cricket. Surprisingly, it would be cricket that gave Trevor Ford his first Welsh cap, representing the principality aged fourteen against a London Schools Under-15 side, excelling as a bowler. On the team that day was another player who dreamt of a life of football: Alf Sherwood, a tremendous full-back who would go on to captain Wales and Cardiff City. It was a real joy for Trevor to be selected, but he knew then that it would only be football for him; in many ways he felt, even at that young age, that he had a bit of unfinished business with the game.

Trevor left school aged fifteen and went to work in the local steelworks as a bogie boy, a tough job that entailed taking hot shells out of the furnace to be made into steel tubes. It was dangerous work as the fire was intense and Trevor would sweat constantly throughout his eight-hour shift. He earned 35 shillings per week, all of which he would give to his mother, who in turn would give him back 5 shillings, which he would spend going to the Vetch to see his heroes in white. Although he was now working, Trevor never gave up on the dream of making it as a professional footballer, and he soon started to play for Tower United, named after his father's cinema. They played in the local league, and as this was men's football, you had to be a tough fifteen-year-old full-back to hold your own. Being 5 foot

10 and slimly built, Trevor fought tooth and nail against older men and proved he could stand his ground. The Tower club started to gain rave reviews and it wasn't long before scouts from different clubs came to Wales to see the team. One of these scouts was legendary Arsenal scout Albert Linden, who had played for Aston Villa, Birmingham City, Charlton and Coventry. He had a reputation of finding some of the country's finest players and at one point found twenty-seven lads who all went on to represent Wales. It was a real coup for the Towerhill side to have him come and watch them, especially when Linden invited forward Frank Davies and Trevor Ford to Cardiff to have a trial for the mighty Arsenal, who were known for having great players like striker Ted Drake, midfielder Cliff Bastin and 'keeper George Swindin, who would later manage Cardiff City in the 1960s.The club was littered with internationals who were all household names. They were managed by George Allison, who had taken over from legendary manager Herbert Chapman after Chapman's sudden death a few years earlier. Alison had steered Arsenal to the League title in 1934/35, the FA Cup in 1935/36 and the title again in 1937/38. Trevor and Frank did well in the trial game so Linden came to Trevor's house to meet his father. He informed Trevor Snr that he had amateur forms for Trevor, but he wanted him to sign them when the threat of war was over, which he believed would only last six months. Then he would be ready to come to Highbury and join Arsenal. A dream come true for both father and son, Trevor Snr was ecstatic and could not believe that Albert Lindon wanted his son to sign for Arsenal, but Trevor had his own views – something he would show throughout his career. Looking at his father, Trevor told him, 'I don't want to leave home yet; I'm too young.' Although he knew this would upset his father, he also knew what he wanted and that was to stay in Swansea. His father said nothing and the matter was dropped. Trevor had shown in that one moment that it would be his way or nothing else; after all, how many youngsters offered that opportunity at fifteen years of age would choose to say no to the League champions and stay working in the steelworks, confident that he would still make it as a player when the time was right for him. However, as 1939 arrived, black clouds descended across Europe, and Britain found itself in another world war.

The town of Swansea was regularly bombarded with night-time air raids, each one hoping to damage the dock and steelworks areas of the town. In total the town would lose 387 of its citizens during the war years. During this time, sixteen-year-old Trevor continued to work in the steelworks and play for Townhill while many local lads had gone overseas to fight for King and Country. Trevor's footballing prowess never diminished and he had certainly not been forgotten, particularly by his local club, so when there was a knock on the door at Merlin Crescent one night and Swansea Town Manager Haydn Green stood there, Trevor knew his dreams had come true and his stubbornness over the Arsenal approach had been vindicated. Haydn Green was a visionary in terms of football management; he had only just been appointed manager to the second-tier club, after spells as manager at Lincoln City, Hull City and Guilford City. But he quickly realised that as the club were scratching around the lower end of the Second Division, and in desperate financial need, the club should tap into the footballing talent of the working-class communities in and around the town. He wanted Swansea Town to become a nursery of talent for these young lads – something that Manchester United's Sir Matt Busby latched onto over ten years later. The club backed Green and invested in the youth of the town, and now he wanted Trevor Ford's signature.

Trevor was seventeen years old when he signed amateur forms for the club in 1940, much to the delight of his father who felt that his son's chance might well have gone after the Arsenal incident. Trevor recalled those initial days at the club:

It was a great day in my young life. I remember being in the dressing room and the smell of the liniment and leather. I sat listening wide-eyed to the talk of football stars of the early years like Jack Fowler, Lot Jones and Ted Vizard. I recall a pleasant feeling of nostalgia and the former centre-half Joe Sykes who was on the ground staff, and players like Billy Sneddon, Frank Squires, Ernie Jones and Roy Paul. They all made me feel welcome at the ground and did their best to teach me something about the game I loved.

Trevor signed professional forms for the club two years later, aged nineteen, after some glowing displays in the heart of the defence for Swansea in the Welsh and the Combination leagues. However, events in Europe meant that in 1943, like many footballers of the day, Trevor's call-up papers arrived on the doorstep, hindering this local lad's rise to the top.

During the war years of 1939–45, the football authorities decided to suspend competitive football. Behind the scenes in football circles a clash was looming between the Players' Union and the Football League. After the Depression of the 1920s and 1930s, attendances at matches had started to rise, and by 1938 the Players' Union was increasing its campaign for a better deal for its members. The maximum wage at the time for players was £10 per week in the season and £6 in the summer, although it is stated by the Professional Footballers Association that only 10 per cent of its members were earning that. The real figure was around £5 in the season and £2 in the summer, and the average attendances at games was around the 20,000 mark. The Players' Union felt that there should be a better distribution of the wealth from the game as at the present state of play all the money in football seemed to go to the directors of the clubs. Although the conflict was the furthest thing from Trevor's mind (at that time he was just a young player), it was an injustice that the outspoken Trevor would be in the very centre of throughout his career. Just a week into the 1939/40 season, the FA suspended all contracts and with it the League ceased to continue, calling a halt to the impending clash between players and its governing body. The government intervened in the cancellation as they saw football as morale boosting for the British people, especially in the difficult times that would lie ahead, so a reorganised regional league was set up of north, south and west, along with a combined regional knockout competition. Although the war would curtail (and in some cases tragically end) football careers, for young lads like Trevor it would give them a platform to shine as youngsters would be given their chance in friendlies and turn out for first teams if regular seasoned players were away with the Army. For Swansea Town, the war would see them move for two years from the Vetch as it had been commandeered for use as an anti-aircraft fortress, so the club had to play their home games on the rugby pitch at St Helens. After receiving his call-up papers, Trevor was posted up to Rhyl in north Wales, where he would join the Royal Artillery. After saying his goodbyes to his family, he left Merlin Crescent and walked to the Swansea station, where he got on a train and headed for a life in uniform. Little did he know how this stint in the Army would shape his footballing career.

2

The Making of a
Number Nine

National Service, or War Service as it was originally known, was
introduced in 1939 by Leslie Hore-Belisha, who was later the
Secretary of State for War in Clement Attlee's Labour government.
The idea to conscript the country's men for two years was certainly
nothing new as it had first been introduced during the First World
War. With the threat of the Nazi Party looming across Europe, the
idea was quickly implemented and it lasted from 1939 right through
until 1960. Originally there would be limited conscription of men
aged between twenty and twenty-two, but after war broke out it
was changed to cover the ages of eighteen to forty-one – in total,
over 2 million conscripts served the country in this time. To the
men of the United Kingdom, National Service was just something
that had to been done. Many look back over that time and think
it was the best two years of their lives, while others couldn't wait
for it to end. For every man who found the experience exciting
and a chance to learn new skills, there would be those who found
it the most tedious couple of years they would ever experience.
For the young Trevor, it was just something that he had to do, so
he kept his head down and got on with it. The train journey from
Swansea to Rhyl was certainly no picnic. Trevor kept himself busy
during the 120-mile journey by staring out of the window as the
Welsh countryside unfolded before his eyes. He was also kept busy
flicking through a deck of cards that he had brought with him,
and of course he tucked into the home-made sandwiches that his
mother Daisy had prepared for his trip. The train seemed to stop
at every station, and with every stop more men got on. Although

Trevor only gave them a passing nod, he guessed that they may well be on their way to do their bit for Britain.

Over four hours had passed when the train pulled into Rhyl station, and as the sun was coming down Trevor was met on the platform by a sergeant with a clipboard who ticked off his name from a list along of conscripts. The men were directed to a large open army truck that was going to be their transport for the thirty-minute trip to the camp. It was only then, as the men piled into the truck, that they started to chat about who they were and where they were from.

Charlie Woods, now well into his nineties and residing in Burnham-on-Sea in the south of England, was a veteran of the park and was there at the same time as Trevor:

> I had come from Bridgend and to be honest the first few days were a bit of a blur. I was a painter and decorator by trade and in all honestly I was not used to being shouted at, but I soon learnt that the best way to deal with it was if it moved salute it and if it didn't paint it. The army camp was at Sunnydale and had been a holiday park, but it had now been taken over by the Army to house around 200 men. The park had a main avenue which was lined either side by small chalets that had slept four holidaymakers at a time. They were of wooden construction and all had a small veranda at the front of them. The park also had an outdoor swimming pool and a bar that was now the mess where we would socialize and have our meals. Within minutes of arriving we were put on the parade ground and told to line up next to each other. The officers then told us what would be expected of us whilse we were in National Service. I remember thinking 'oh well, at least I'm not abroad' like some of my mates were. We were then allocated chalets, which now held eight men to a room, and told to report to the shower block, two chalets at a time. We were given a pay book as we would be getting 9 shillings a day and they would be stopping us half a crown for barrack damage. Then we were allocated our irons, which was our knife, fork and spoon, and they told us if you lost them you could use your hands. And at last our uniform was given to us all folded and one size fitted all. After our showers we were given our inoculations and then a standard haircut.

This was something the young Trevor never forgot, as he was very fond of his thick-swept, black hair. He mentioned in various interviews throughout his career about that moment: 'I was kitted out, given a devastating haircut and three swift injections, then paraded on the barrack square like a shot.' The disciplined routine would have come as a major shock to some men, but Trevor took it all in his stride as he had known discipline, particularly in his quest to be a professional footballer. The days would be planned out: rise at 0600, wash, shave, polish boots, and be in the cookhouse for breakfast at 0700. Breakfast was usually porridge then the men had to be on parade at 0800. During the day they would learn squad drills, map-reading, work on rifles, keep fit and basic soldering, and when they were not doing that they would be painting the whole of the camp. Trevor took to Army life, especially the keep fit regime. Every day he worked out in the gym as he thought it was a perfect way to set himself up for his return to Swansea. Charlie Woods again gave an insight into how popular he was with the rest of his battalion:

> Trevor was well liked. He always shared his cigarettes and was never short when it came to buying his round in the mess. On the odd occasion we ventured into the town of Rhyl, he was always popular with the ladies as he had this mop of black hair and film-star looks. Even then he looked better than we did in that godawful uniform, which was made to fit just one size. You could tell he was ambitious; often he would talk about owning a big house, having a car and being the best player for Swansea Town. I followed his career and I could not understand it when papers said he was trouble. I knew him at that time for a couple of months and he was a great lad.

Trevor longed to get the ball at his feet again, so when a sergeant barked 'Parade for football tomorrow. Let's have some volunteers. Those who want a game, one pace forward march', he thought he had died and gone to Heaven. Trevor puffed out his chest and took a step forward, informing the sergeant that he was in fact a full-back on Swansea Town's books. 'Who the bloody hell are Swansea Town?' shouted the sergeant. The sergeant looked at the list of volunteers and their allocated positions and informed Trevor that he already had four full-backs and he didn't want another. With that, Trevor was dismissed with everybody else. Plainly this was a crushing blow to the young Trevor and he struggled to stay positive as he walked back to the chalet, thinking that maybe he was really destined to see out his life in the steelworks when his Army life was over. With that, a corporal who was also a PT instructor called Trevor back. What he said next would move Trevor's footballing career into a completely different level: 'You're a professional footballer. You should be able to play anywhere, Ford.' Trevor nodded. 'Right, then you can turn out as centre forward for tomorrow's game.' Trevor was just happy to have been picked, and it wasn't until he was lying on his bunk that he started to think, 'Can I really play centre forward?' Little did he know that he had all the raw talent to become the costliest player in British football and one of the most feared centre forwards the game has ever produced.

It was on a rain-swept pitch that Trevor Ford first put on the number nine shirt in the inter-unit match. And although he started off very apprehensive, he soon settled into his role, making runs and being a physical presence to the opposing back four. With the game at 0-0, the inside forward wrong-footed the centre half and pushed a lovely ball into the path of the oncoming Ford, who hit a ferocious shot that screamed into the top corner of the goal. Later in the second half, Trevor bravely stuck his head into a melee of players and headed his and the team's second goal. The game ended with Trevor's team 2-0 victors, and all the applause from officers and squaddies was for the dark-haired Welshman. Later, as Trevor laid in his bunk, he started to realise that centre forward was definitely the position for him in the future, and that's where he wanted to play, whether Swansea liked it or not. Trevor would play regularly for his unit against other camps, and although this was more of an exercise to keep the men happy, Trevor approached every game as though he was playing for Wales. He just could not stop scoring, and his reputation grew as a tough yet talented player among the armed forces. After around six months Trevor was moved from Rhyl to an anti-aircraft unit in Colchester. This move turned out to be perfect for the young striker as he was free on the weekends. Obviously it was too far to travel back to Swansea, but one corporal, who was a massive fan of this bustling striker and had connections at Leyton Orient Football Club in the East End of London, arranged for Trevor to play some games for the club on a weekend. Trevor was thrilled by this request as it was worth £2 a game (equivalent to £20 today), and that was more than he was getting for a week in the Army. In total Trevor played four games for Orient and scored three goals in the process. He was thrilled to be back in the footballing world and to be playing against other professionals. These games convinced him that he had made the right choice and could hold his own playing centre forward against accomplished defenders rather than squaddie teams. Alf Williams, a lifelong Orient fan, remembers stories his late father told of Trevor:

> Dad followed Orient all his life and that's why I loved them. He always told a story about watching Trevor Ford play for Orient during the war. Dad was about fourteen years old at the time and Orient played Brentford at Brisbane Road. They won 2-0 and Dad remembers this young dark head forward who was down in the programme as a guest scoring two goals with his head. He used to say that he gave the Brentford defence a torrid time that afternoon, and in particularly an Irish defender called Bill Gorman who was experienced and went on to play for his country, Trevor tore him apart and poor old Billy certainly knew he had been in a game. Weeks later Trevor Ford scored against Portsmouth. Dad followed his career since then and he always used to say he wished Orient could've bought him.

Leyton Orient's loss was always going to be Swansea Town's gain as there was only one club for Trevor. Turning out for Orient and playing regular football was a dream come true for Trevor and he enjoyed his time in Essex, but unfortunately he would receive some worrying news. One afternoon Trevor was called from his dormitory and ordered to go to the orderly room. He was then told that his mother Daisy was undergoing a serious operation back in Swansea. Trevor was granted two weeks' special leave to go home and see his mother. He left that night and caught the train from Colchester to Paddington station, and then on to Swansea. It was an arduous trip that saw him arrive back at Merlin Crescent in the early hours of the morning. His father and siblings were thrilled to see him, but obviously it would have been better in different circumstances. Trevor's dad made a pot of tea and the family chatted for hours about Daisy who was suffering from a kidney problem. Trevor felt assured that she was over the worst and he could not wait to go and see her in the morning. He thought it better to tell his father about his success as a centre forward after he had seen that Mum was okay with his own eyes. The family visited Daisy and she was thrilled to see her Trevor in the flesh.

While Daisy was recovering and Trevor's leave was coming to an end, he received a telegram from the Army which explained that in light of recent personal circumstances he was being transferred to an army base in Neath. Trevor could not believe his luck. He was now just 12 miles from his home in Swansea and with a bit of wheeling and dealing with his fellow squaddies for twenty-four-hour passes, he could offer his services back to Swansea Town. They welcomed him home with open arms, with Haydn Green telling him that he had heard some great things about his exploits as a centre forward, particularly from a contact he had in London who had seen his performances for Leyton Orient. He also remarked on how he had grown physically and had become more muscular during his time away. On his return to the Royal Artillery barracks in Neath, he was contacted by phone, asking if he could turn out for Swansea against Aberaman in the West Regional Cup qualifier on the forthcoming Saturday. A quick ask around among his colleagues and Trevor got himself a forty-eight-hour pass for the game.

The game was at the Vetch and it was a cold January afternoon. Around 1,500 people had arrived to watch the game, one of whom was Trevor's father. Haydn Green had a quick word with young Trevor and told him to put himself about and cause problems. The Swansea team was mostly made up of guests and youngsters like Trevor. The game was an end-to-end affair, and Haydn Green could see that he was a bit rough around the edges but he had a physical presence to his game now and he was fearless, something Green later stated: 'You could not coach that. Trevor had it in abundance.' The Swans won the game 2-0 and although Trevor had a few chances, he didn't score, and he was disappointed with himself. Green explained to him that he was not just there to score goals, but also there to help others achieve goals, but nineteen-year-old Trevor just nodded, knowing he would do better next time. He walked home with his father, who was thrilled to see him play; the two of them dissected the match all the way to Merlin Cresent.

   That night Trevor went over his game and remembered what David Benyon had instilled in him about working as a member of the team and letting the ball do the work. With Army commitments it would be April before he would pull on the shirt again. He had trained at the club at every chance he had when on leave, but actual games for the Swans were few and far between because of the war. This time he got a four-day pass as he was asked to play against Cardiff City at Ninian Park and then local team Lovell's Athletic two days later. The derby game against Cardiff attracted 2,500 fans to Ninian Park, although the rivalry between the two clubs was certainly not as fierce as it is today; in fact when Cardiff beat Arsenal to win the FA Cup in 1927, many residents of Swansea travelled to Cardiff to see them bring the cup home. Again both teams had many of their stars missing and the clubs were relying on youngsters eager to make the grade and a few 'guests' thrown in, but Cardiff had a strong team that included Alf Sherwood, who was Trevor's teammate when they both played cricket for Wales. Cardiff started the game well and were 2-0 up deep into the first half. Trevor had done himself justice and was getting well and truly stuck into the Cardiff back four. Then just before half-time, Swansea had a corner and Trevor rose above two Cardiff defenders to bury the ball into the net with his head. In the second half Swansea took control and scored another four goals, two of them made by Trevor. The Swans eventually ran out 5-2 winners. As the team ran off, Alf Sherwood shook Trevor's hand and told him that he was some player. He remarked on how he had 'beefed' himself up in the Army and how he played like a man possessed. The two of them left the field mud-splattered and waiting for a hot bath in the changing rooms. Haydn Green was delighted with the youngster's display and immediately gave him the number nine shirt for the forthcoming games against Lovell's Athletic. Lovell's Athletic were a top team at the time; they were essentially a work's team that derived from the Lovell's sweets factory in the Newport area. During the war years Newport County did not field a side, so Lovell's became the top team in the area, attracting many top players. The game against Lovell's stuck in Trevor's mind many years later, not only for his two goals in the 4-2 win, but the influence of two players who played with him in that Swansea team. It was the first time he had played with future Swansea,

Manchester City and Wales legend Roy Paul. He was one player that had a big effect on him:

> Roy was a tough lad. He never said much, but one look at you could floor you. He led by example and never shirked a challenge and I admired him for that. He was a couple of years older than me but he played like an old pro. His tackling and ball skills were up there with the best.

Another player who Trevor never forgot was one of Swansea's guests for the match, Stan Mortensen, who went on to be the only player to score a hat-trick in an FA Cup final when his Blackpool side beat Bolton 4-3. He also played twenty-five times for England and scored twenty-three goals in the process. Trevor recalls the encounter:

> I had a real shock when I found out who would be playing outside right with me, the brilliant Stan Mortensen. What an education it was to play with him. His skill and distribution highlighted what David Benyon had drummed into me when I was a kid about letting the ball do the work. Stan made my job as a centre forward so much easier with his clever passing into space and how he could draw defenders out of position. He was a master.

Trevor finished the 1942/43 with four appearances and three goals. Although the next two seasons would see Trevor making just nine appearances due to the war, he still managed seven goals in that time. With the end of the war and the return to the Football League fixtures, as far as Haydn Green was concerned he had truly unearthed Swansea Town's and even Wales' next centre forward.

3

Building a Reputation

There was certainly an air of anticipation throughout the whole of football as the 1945/46 season arrived. Although many players were still in the Army – Trevor included – the clubs, players and of course supporters felt that with the end of hostilities throughout Europe people could finally enjoy themselves and try and get back to normal without forgetting the terrible loss to the country that the Second World War brought. Trevor was still based in Neath with the Royal Artillery, but he could now commit fully to hopefully playing every game for the Swans. He certainly wanted to prove that the war had been just a hiccup in his footballing carreer. He had played local teams from the South West and now wanted to show the whole of the footballing world who Trevor Ford was. The war had been kind to Trevor: he was blessed with not being posted abroad like many of his generation, and physically he had certainly matured and become a man, which helped his game tremendously.

For Swansea Town they were joining the Football League south, which included all the southern, teams in the country and as far north as Derby and Nottingham. It really was a transitional league, billed as the 'Victory League' and a forerunner to the league tables that would return the following year. The club over the years had certainly not pulled up any trees; they had spent the majority of the time in the lower regions of the football pyramid with the odd cup run and Welsh Cup win. But Swansea had always produced good players and played in what was 'the Swansea way', which was a pass-and-move-type game. For this season Haydn Green realized that his biggest asset in the forthcoming season would be the bustling no-nonsense unknown Trevor Ford up front, a player who thrived on the ball in the air and the chance to attack the back four, including the 'keeper, whenever he got the chance. Green wanted to produce a quick, young team that was, for the majority, comprised of local talent, but still the demands of National Service compromised his overall vision, as some players were still not available. The first game of the 1945/46 season was away to West Bromwich Albion and the Swansea line up included Gilchrist in goal and consisted of a back four of Davies, Fischer, Hodgson and Weston. In midfield were Allen, Jones, Burns and Millchip, with Ford and Gallon up front. The team had a few debutants, in particular big Reg Weston at centre half. The team also included Frank Burns at wing half, who was a tough tackling player, and Ernie Jones who was a tricky winger whose job was to get the ball out to Trevor as quick as he could. There were 18,000 people packed into the Hawthorns to see the first match, and as the teams ran out, Trevor certainly felt he had arrived. Swansea were the better team in the first half, with Trevor making his presence known to the Albion two centre halfs, Witcomb and Gripton. They in turn reciprocated the favour by diving in on Trevor's ankle just to let him know they were there. Trevor was also spoken to by referee Mr Liffe for fouling the 'keeper Harris. This was certainly a vision of what was to come later in his career. The first half ended 0-0 and manager Green was pleased with his team. Early in the second half there were injuries to Swansea full-back Davies and striker Millchip, but as there were no subs back then they struggled through. This would signal the end for the Swans as they were effectively down to nine men. Albion went 2-0 up and then a ball was pushed up to Trevor, who fought off the two Albion defenders, giving himself a chance to shoot. From 20 yards he thundered a right-foot shot into the net, giving the Albion 'keeper no chance. It was just a glimmer as the Swans tired near the end and conceded two more goals, running out 4-1 losers. The disappointment was plain to see in the young Swansea side, but Trevor was pleased to have recorded his first 'proper' goal for the club. He got praise also from the *Western Mail* newspaper who wrote, 'Ford held the line together well considering the fact that he got a nasty knock early in the game.' To be recognized by the newspaper really cheered the young striker up, and although the club lost he enjoyed the odd wave from supporters when he was walking around Swansea.

The following two fixtures would see defeat again for the Swans as they lost 5-0 to Portsmouth and 4-2 against WBA in front of 8,000 at the Vetch, Trevor again scoring one of the Swansea goals. Haydn Green was struggling with injuries and had to rejig his team for the trip to Aston Villa the following week. Full-back Davies was out injured, along with striker Millchip. He moved some players out of position and added 'guest' Howard Prescott from Hull City to the attack.

The moment the young Swansea team arrived through the gates at Villa Park they could see that this was a club steeped in rich tradition. The ground itself dwarfed the Vetch and could hold 75,000 supporters. Aston Villa had been one of the top sides before the war and were certainly going to carry on that mantle afterwards. The club contained players of the calibre of George Cummings, Ronnie Starling and George Edwards. Trevor and his teammates were like kids as they walked into the changing rooms; they could be heard 'oohing and aahing' at the facilities before Haydn Green's loud voice concentrated their minds on the game ahead. They ran out to 25,000 fans and it was certainly one of the biggest crowds some of them had played in front of, and it also showed how popular the game was getting after the war years. Aston Villa showed their class early on, gaining a 2-0 lead, but credit to the young Swansea lads, they never let their heads drop and were rewarded when Trevor was tripped in the box by Villa defender Cummings. Trevor showed tremendous maturity by grabbing the ball and placing it down on the spot before there was any discussion over who was going to take it. He stood there with the whole of Villa Park hoping he would miss, then he smashed it off to Villa 'keeper Wakeman's left. He ran back to the centre circle, giving handshakes to his teammates. Just before half-time, Villa went further ahead and went into the interval 3-1 up. Again Trevor was battling against the defenders and the 'keeper like an old pro and looked well above his years. His enthusiasm was rewarded when he won the ball on the edge of the box and laid a lovely pass to Frank Burns, who was running from midfield. Frank crashed the ball home to make it 3-2. Villa showed their class and stepped up a gear, scoring three more goals before Trevor headed another goal for the Swans. At the final whistle Villa player Ronnie Starling ran over to Trevor and shook his hand, congratulating him on a fine display. The gesture meant a lot to the young Trevor. The 25,000 Villa supporters had witnessed a wonderful game and they all applauded as the teams left the field. The crowd had also seen a young Welsh forward give a display that would send them home talking about him. He had not gone unnoticed in the Villa directors' box. The *Birmingham Mail* newspaper commented: 'In young Trevor Ford, Swansea have a youngster well above his years. He was ferocious in the tackle and could go to the very top.'

Results were starting to weigh heavy on manager Green's mind as the Swans suffered their fifth defeat in a row after losing 1-0 to Millwall, but he believed in his young Swansea team and knew that the following season he would have a lot of his players back from National Service. At that moment his thoughts turned to his next opponents who happened to be Villa again, this time at the Vetch.

The match with Villa at the Vetch was, in Trevor's words, 'the greatest thrill of my young life'. A strong Villa side, particularly defensively, came to the Vetch and were in no uncertain terms torn apart by the young striker from Towerhill. It was a close game as Swansea won 5-4, but the hat-trick Ford scored against some of the top players of the day made the footballing world sit up and take notice of this youngster in south Wales, even this early into the season. Ford bossed the Villa back four, and it got to a stage where, with Ford's superior aerial presence and the threat of getting a whack, Villa 'keeper Wakeman refused to come for some crosses, much to the dismay of his defence. As the game ended, 15,000 Welshman rose to their feet to clap off Swansea and their first win of the season, and Trevor's first hat-trick in football. Villa and the whole of the Villa defence, including 'keeper Wakeman, who had certainly had enough of him over ninety minutes, patted him on the back and wished him well. Trevor also remembers that Scotland defender George Cummings shook him by the hand and said, 'Score anymore goals like that and I will personally see to it that you don't come to Villa Park.' They both laughed as they left the field. The newspapers again had a field day, commenting, 'Sharp shooting Ford whose second half hat-trick was one of the most spectacular things in this football feast, had to be seen to be believed.' It was plain to see that there was one club that would be looking at this youngster a bit more closely. He was certainly gaining the star treatment in and around Swansea as young supporters followed him around and wanted his autograph. All of this attention he loved, but he would also get the odd comment from fans who thought his game was just about fouling the 'keeper, and they would say he wasn't really a player and shouldn't be playing for the Swans as he was nothing like the gentleman of yesteryear who played for them, men like Jack Fowler or Joe Sykes, all great players from the 1920s. Comments like this did not appear to bother Trevor as his own nature meant that he would give as good back, but inside it did hurt and there was always a feeling that even in those early days he wasn't appreciated by some.

The Swans continued their erratic form, but for Trevor was building a formidable reputation up front, battling and scoring against the very top teams and players at the time. Trevor was always willing to improve his game and when great players were in opposition, he continued to study what they did. What Trevor never realized was that a lot of these players were keen to see the youngster from south Wales in action. He continued scoring and was fast becoming the talk of football as he notched another hat-trick against Tommy Lawton's Chelsea, a goal against Derby County, a team that included Raich Carter and Peter Doherty, and a goal against Stan Cullis at Wolverhampton Wanderers. Trevor certainly made an immediate impact on Cullis, who at the time was an established England international. In the week leading up to the Wolves game, his teammates were telling him that Cullis was letting everybody know that he would certainly put this young upstart from south Wales in his place. This 'wind up' by the Swansea players was growing and growing and young Trevor was getting more and more angry about what Cullis had said about him, oblivious to the fact that it was all nonsense.

When the game kicked off, Swansea had possession and the ball was played upfield, only to be taken by the Wolves' defence, where Cullis was in possession. He had no more than seconds on the ball before Trevor dropped his shoulder and crashed into Cullis. The challenge was perfectly legal in those days, but Stan Cullis, England international, found himself in a heap against the wooden stand that ran along the touchline. Cullis was stretchered off and missed most of the season through injury. In the dressing room some of the lads asked him why he had gone in so hard on Cullis, but Trevor replied, 'Well I showed him I wasn't about to be pushed around.' Nobody had the heart to tell him it was a wind-up. Trevor's reputation as a tough competitor was certainly growing. He knew he had raw talent, but he openly admitted that he was in no way the finished article like some of the players he was playing against. When the season came to an end the Swans had finished seventeenth in a league that was won by Birmingham City, with Midland rivals Aston Villa runners-up. Trevor had scored forty-one goals in forty-three matches, a record that will certainly stand for a very long time.

Trevor used the summer to come to terms with leaving the Army and settling back down to life. He was certainly the talk of the estate, but the people of Townhill never let it go to his head – he was still young Trevor. He kept fit by having a kick about with the local kids in the park and also playing his other love, cricket. During the summer there were all sorts of rumours about Swansea's number one asset, but he just dismissed it as 'paper talk'. Back at the club, Haydn Green had now got most of his big players back, players like Roy Paul and Frank Squires. Green realized that after last season's campaign, he needed to add some steel and experience into his young side as they embarked on a season in the Football League's Second Division. Again, as with last year, their opponents would be WBA. Green's team had local lad Jack Parry in goal and included Briddon, Fisher, Paul, Weston, Burns, Jones, Squires, Ford, Haines and Comley. The steel was added by Paul, who was a Rhondda lad and had just come out of the Marines. He was a colossus on the field and led by example; the half back line of Paul, Weston and Burns would become legendary over the years. Trevor could not wait for the game as he now felt that the team was more equipped than last year; he was very excited about the number of goals he could score.

It was disappointing start to the season all round for the Swans. Although they had held their own in a tight game, they lost 3-2 and had Frank Burns sent off for arguing with the referee over whether WBA's third goal had crossed the line. Trevor had played his heart out as usual, roughing up the back four and causing them to make a mistake and score an own goal. He still felt that if he did not score then he had not played well. A further defeat at the hands of Southampton followed before he got his chance on the big stage, away at Newcastle United. Newcastle were one of the top sides at the time and 53,000 fans crammed into St James' Park with 8,000 locked outside, again proving how top-level football was missed in the war years. Games like this were made for Trevor: he loved running out with 53,000 Geordies praying that he had a stinker and giving him stick. He felt ten feet tall and he puffed his chest out ready to do battle against the likes of defender Joe Harvey and legendary forward Jackie Milburn. The game was 0-0 at half-time, but Trevor had already had a ball bounce off the crossbar and land on the goal line. He had fought and scrapped for every chance. Early in the second half Newcastle got the breakthrough from striker Woodburn. With the game drifting away from Swansea, Trevor once again outjumped what seemed to be the whole of the Newcastle defence and crashed a header into the net with five minutes to go, gaining the club a well-deserved draw.

The first win of the season came at home to Nottingham Forest. Trevor scored in the 3-2 win, but also took a nasty knock to the shin. Although it required treatment after the game, it did not keep him out of the following match against Bradford Park Avenue at the Vetch, although it was a match I'm sure he wished he had missed. Bradford had taken thirteen hours to arrive at the Vetch so you would assume they would be there for the taking, but unfortunately nobody told their maverick player, Len Shackleton. Bradford destroyed Swansea 6-1 with Shackleton scoring a hat-trick. It was a tough afternoon for the Swansea number nine as he was also barracked by a section of the Swansea crowd who shouted 'play fair, Ford' as they did not agree with his rough style of play towards the 'keeper and the defenders. Arthur Tanner, who has supported the Swans for over sixty years, tells us how Trevor was not his father's favourite as a player:

> My Dad was a lifelong fan. He saw all the greats through the years but he openly used to tell me that he never rated Ford. As far as my dad was concerned he belonged on a rugby pitch. He thought he was a dirty player with all his attacking of rival 'keepers. He used to say he would shout at ford any chance he got from the terraces. Dad thought he wasn't a gentleman on the pitch.

A move to the number eight spot followed for the game against Tottenham Hotspur as Cliff Passmore was given Trevor's number nine shirt as part of Haydn Green's tactics. Although Trevor got on with it, he hated having it taken off him as he saw it as the top striker's shirt and any other forwards' number was there to help the number nine get goals. Defeat against Spurs followed and Trevor missed the next game against Burnley due to a recurrence of an ankle injury. But a move back to number nine saw a run of three games and three goals for Ford.

As the season went on Trevor was not as prolific as the first season, and this was mainly due to bouts of injury. In addition, the opposing clubs had begun to realise what they were dealing with and Trevor was no longer the surprise package. As 1946 came to a close the Swans found themselves at the wrong half of the table. Trevor had played fifteen games and scored eight goals. Looking at the future, it was clear that Swansea were never in the position to win the league, especially when trying to compete with the likes of Newcastle United, Manchester City, Burnley and Birmingham City, who could all afford big squads. So it was an FA Cup run that the Swansea board felt they could do well in. With this in mind, the club decided that, with a home game against Newcastle United coming up, along with an FA Cup game at home with Gillingham, they would take the players off to the Pembrokeshire countryside. With the Newcastle game on the horizon, the players stayed in a remote farmhouse for a week. The hosts and the food were enjoyable, but boredom soon set in for the cooped-up bunch of footballers, who had left their home comforts when training finished. It was never going to be good for morale as teammates began to get on each other's nerves. In his book, Trevor recalled how,

> There was a radiogram in the farmhouse but they had only one record which was Frank Sinatra singing 'Nancy with the laughing eyes'. This was played over and over again until I would've willingly smashed a ball right through Nancy's smiling eyes. The song almost drove me nuts.

With tensions high, the team finished the week and headed to the Vetch for the match against Newcastle. Before the game, Trevor announced to Haydn Green that he would not be going to that godawful place again; as far as he was concerned he would be better in his own bed and train at the Vetch. He told Green he found the whole experience a misery and that it never got him in the mood for the game ahead. The game ended with a defeat for Swansea 2-1 with Trevor getting the Swans' goal and that man Shackleton getting one of the goals for his new club, Newcastle. After the game Green announced that the team must report to the Vetch at 8 a.m. on Monday for the trip to Pembrokeshire as preparation for the FA Cup game with Gillingham. Trevor responded by telling Green that he was not going. Green just nodded and the rest of the Swansea lads looked around at the floor not sure what to say, with Roy Paul being the only one who said, 'He might have a point, Haydn.' Haydn shook his head, so Trevor left, and true to his word he woke up at 9 a.m. then reported to the Vetch for training at 10.30, knowing that the team would have left for the countryside. As he entered the ground with his bag over his shoulder, Haydn Green, who had stayed at the Vetch with the intention of seeing Trevor, met him. Green told him to go home until the matter was resolved. With that he swiftly turned around and went back home while Haydn Green spoke to the board. This was one of the first acts of defiance from Trevor and these were the incidents that led to his 'Troublesome Trevor' tag. Whether it was his big-time Charlie attitude, as some have said, or just the strength of character that he showed his father in not going to Arsenal all those years ago, his decision set the wheels in motion for a change in his life.

News spread like wildfire throughout football and the following few days the papers were full of inquiries about the services of the new young centre forward from the likes of Brentford, Fulham, Huddesfield, Sheffield Wednesday, Liverpool, Derby County and, obviously, Aston Villa. Trevor certainly enjoyed the attention and started to think about his future, and he quickly realized that there was money to be made at these clubs. If they wanted him they would have to pay for him. These clubs could give provide him with excellent facilities, a chance to play with top players and the chance to make him a top player himself. He realized that the £15-a-week he was on at Swansea could certainly be added to by these big clubs in all sorts of ways. He mixed with other footballers and in the Swansea dressing room there were always rumours about what and how certain teams were paying their players. A move could get him all the things he wanted as a kid: his own house, a car and the opportunity to look after his family. Football was all about scoring goals and he had the talent to do that. So with that in mind he pre-empted any decision from Swansea by going to the chairman, Mr Freedman, and telling him he wanted to leave the club. Freedman told him it was a misunderstanding and the club did not want to lose him. But Trevor stood firm and Freedman said he would speak to the board and be in touch. The Swansea board met deep into the night and the dilemma was that they needed money, as always yet Ford was their star player but his act of defiance could not be good for the team. If they kept him they would have an unhappy player who would think he could do what he liked, and if they sold him they could put money in the bank and possibly buy another player. Trevor spoke to his family, who supported him 100 per cent in whatever he wanted to do, but there was still no news from Swansea. It was in the middle of the week when Trevor sat in the local cinema watching the latest release when an attendant tapped him on the shoulder and whispered that there was a message for him at reception. Trevor opened the note which read, 'Mr. Ford will you please see Mr. Billy Smith of Aston Villa in the Mackworth Hotel Swansea at 9pm tomorrow.' He looked up and whispered to himself, 'It looks like Villa then.' His time at Swansea had ended and, providing he liked what Villa had to say, his future lay in one of the biggest clubs in England. This suited Trevor down to the ground.

4

The Villa

The Mackworth Hotel was a very large, grand Victorian building. It stood around seven storeys high with ornate iron railings around the balcony of the first floor. Below it stood retail outlets, but there was no hiding the fact that the large double-fronted door was the way in to a very opulent building, an imposing structure on Swansea's main high street. Inside was just as formidable, with high ceilings and chandeliers everywhere. As Trevor entered the building he looked all around at customers in expensive suits and dresses being waited on hand and foot, and in that one instance he felt at home. He felt excited thinking of what lay ahead and knew that if he liked what Villa had to say, he would have to get use to buildings like this. His mind was brought back to the present when he heard Haydn Green say 'Hi Trevor, they are waiting for us through here.' The two men walked into a large room and as the large oak door opened, Trevor could see two men sat at a table. Both got up as Haydn Green introduced them as Mr Fred Normansell, chairman of Aston Villa, and Mr Billy Smith, secretary. Both got up to shake his hand. Trevor was shocked to see the chairman attend the meeting. Fred Normansell ordered tea for everybody and after the pleasantries of asking how they all got here and how they were keeping, Haydn Green got down to business. He explained to Trevor that Aston Villa were prepared to pay Swansea Town the fee they wanted for him, but he pointed out that Trevor had the last say if he did not want to go. Deep down Trevor knew that it was all about the clubs really, as they were the ones who owned his registration. So even if you wanted to stay, the club held all the cards. He also remarked that Villa were a team of wonderful traditions – it was a remark that led Trevor to think that Mr Green and the Swansea board were desperate for him to sign for Villa. The actual figure for the transfer was £9,500 plus Aston Villa forward Tommy Dodds. Billy Smith then remarked that the club would be very happy for Trevor to sign as they saw him as a wonderful up-and-coming player who could become better at Villa. He then went on to say that Trevor would be receiving his £10 signing on fee when he got to Aston Villa and that he would certainly not lose out financially by making the move. Mr Normansell then pushed the papers across the table to Trevor and produced a fountain pen from his suit pocket. 'What do you say then Trevor?' Trevor looked through the contract and signed. With this Mr Normansell got up from the chair and ordered whiskeys all round.

After a few drinks Trevor left with Haydn Green, and as they both stood in the warmth of the foyer they shook hands. Although they had not really seen eye to eye in the past months, Trevor certainly knew that it was Haydn's belief in him that had got him on the road to football stardom. Haydn wished him luck and Trevor wished him the same. As the two men went in to the cold night air they looked at each other with mutual respect and nodded. Their time together was now over.

Aston Villa have always been a massive and iconic club in Britain; as one of the founding member clubs of the Football, League, they can boost a rich history. When Trevor signed in 1947, the club had won six league titles and six FA Cups and were playing in Division One, attracting crowds in the region of 50,000 to Villa Park. Former player Alex Massie managed them and the tough Scot was in the process of rebuilding this great club. They, like many teams, had lost players to the war, but they had not had the foresight as some clubs like Manchester United and Wolverhampton Wanderers had in investing in youth. Villa's team was ageing and they decided to spend for the future. With Trevor's impressive start to the season, Massie and the board decided to invest the majority of their transfer budget on the man from Wales.

Villa Park was certainly an impressive sight as the young Welshman entered the ground for the first time. Armed with his kit bag full of washing and his boots, Trevor took a deep breath and sucked it all in. The huge wrought-iron gates, inscribed with Aston Villa Football Club, opened up and Trevor could see the huge red-brick stadium in front of him. The expansive lawns and flower beds of the administrative headquarters looked like something out of a palace, not that this lad from Swansea had ever been near a palace in his young life. Secretary Billy Smith and manager Alex Massie greeted him, and he was then led to the changing rooms to meet the rest of the team, who were congregating after training. Alex Massie signed for Villa as a player in 1935 in a £6,000 deal that brought him down from Heart of Midlothian. Already a Scotland international, he was renowned for his patience and skill on the ball. A mesmeric dribbler and a superb passer of the ball, he was a vital part of the promotion team of the 1937/38 season. He later became captain and then, after Jimmy Hogan's departure as manager in 1939, he got the hot seat at Villa Park.

Trevor walked into a bustling noise of laughter, singing and shouting, but within seconds it fell silent. Massie introduced him to the side and then he left, obviously leaving Trevor to socialise with the lads. The team were certainly a real mix – young and old, long-time Villa players and players who had just signed. One of the first players who came up to Trevor was George Edwards. Edwards shook him firmly by the hand and welcomed him to the side. It was a marvellous gesture by the Villa centre forward as the whole of the team knew that the man from Swansea would be taking George's number nine shirt for the rest of his time at Villa. Edwards apparently had already been informed that he would be switched to the right wing to accommodate Trevor. Another player eager to speak to Trevor was Johnny Dixon. Johnny was a young winger from County Durham who had played for Villa before the war, and like Trevor he was now in the process of getting his chance in the team. Frank Moss jumped up also to shake his hand. Frank was a towering centre half who had arrived from Sheffield Wednesday before the war, and he introduced full-back Harry Parkes, who was a local lad and a bit of a comedian. All the lads told Trevor that if he wanted a few quid Harry was the man to get the racing tips off. In all, Trevor felt at home and nobody made him feel uncomfortable regarding the way he had left Swansea. It was a whole different world when it came to training at Villa; at

Swansea there would be running, a quick match and then home – if you wanted to do anything else it was up to you. At the Villa there was all sorts of stuff going on: forwards would be taken away to practice scoring; defenders would be constantly working on corners; players would play five-a-side games, and also do work in a state-of-the-art gymnasium; and after training the players would be taken to lunch at a nearby hotel or maybe play a round of golf to finish the day. In all it was clear that this was a big football club. Trevor's signing certainly caught the attention of the fans as they all knew what type of forward he was – and that was one in the mould of two of their previous greats, Harry Hampton and Tom 'Pongo' Waring. Hampton had terrorized defences during the early 1900; he scored 242 goals from 373 appearances and he was a burly centre forward who took no prisoners, especially when it came to goalkeepers. He was an aggressive, whole-hearted player, unpopular with opposing fans but loved by his own. He won the Cup twice with Villa, along with the Championship, and was capped four times for England. Waring was and still is the greatest goalscorer in Aston Villa's rich history. He joined the club in 1928 from Tranmere Rovers, and although he was quick-footed and skilful, this Scouser had an imposing presence in the box, which he used to his advantage. Like Trevor, he had a reputation for doing things his way. Former strike partner Billy Walker once said of him, 'There were no rules for Pongo, he just did his own thing. Nobody at the club could do anything with him'. Waring scored 167 goals for the club in 226 appearances.

Trevor made his debut against Arsenal at Highbury. He made a wry smile to himself when he found out it was Arsenal because of the conversation he had with Albert Lindon all those years ago at Townhill when Albert wanted to sign him for the London club. The club had travelled down on the Friday night by train and were staying in a hotel in north London. And as the team's coach inched its way through the hordes of fans, Trevor loved being part of top-level football. His debut that afternoon to be honest was a decent one: he put himself about, harassing the Arsenal defence, and got a few contacts against the 'keeper just to let him know he was there. The 50,000 home crowd became evermore restless, especially when Trevor won the ball on the edge of the box, turned and let fly with a rasping left-foot shot only for the Arsenal 'keeper to fumble and Villa's Smith put the club 1-0 up. Villa gained a second in the second half when Dickie Dorsett struck from the edge of the box. It was a great start for Villa and Trevor, but typical of him, he did not feel the joy 100 per cent, as his name was not on the scoresheet. Sure he had done his bit, but to Trevor a centre forward must score as this was his job. Villa's style of play was a little different to Swansea, where the Welsh club got the ball quickly to Trevor and made use of his power and speed. Villa got the ball around the pitch better, but in that first game every time the ball got up to him, he found he would be closely marshalled by two Arsenal centre-backs who had been given time to regroup. But Trevor just looked forward to his home debut against Blackpool the following week. The young Welshman hit the ground running at Villa Park. He was mobbed as he tried to get into the ground by autograph hunters and people wanting to welcome him to the club and shake his hand. Eventually he got into the dressing room where he found Harry Parkes had hid his shorts in the shower. Trevor laughed as Harry shouted 'where's your shorts Trevor?' It was obvious there would be no big-time Charlie persona at this club and Trevor loved it. Alex Massie gave his team talk. Most of the players would be smoking cigarettes, particularly Trevor, who was a ten-a-day man. Then the bell rang and it was time to go out to the pitch. Everyone wished each other well and then they ran out. The noise of 35,000 Villa fans resonated around the ground and again Trevor felt invincible. The game ended 1-1 with Trevor smashing home the Villa goal. It was fantastic to get off the mark, especially in front of those passionate fans.

Again the style of play meant that Trevor had to be more patient in waiting for the ball, which was not easy for him – he wanted to tell them to get it up to him quicker, but he kept his mouth shut as he knew that if he got his chance he would score. Plus, he did not really want to rock the boat at his new club. With his first goal behind him, Trevor went on a run, scoring both goals in a 2-0 win away at Brentford and getting one of the Villa consolation goals in a 3-2 defeat at Portsmouth. An injury picked up in the Portsmouth game kept him out of the side for the next few games until his return in March against Chelsea at Villa Park. Villa won the game 2-0. Although not fully fit, Trevor got on the scoresheet, scoring from a Villa corner. He missed the next few games and returned against Sunderland at Villa Park in April. There were 30,000 in Villa Park that afternoon to see Villa tear Sunderland apart with their quick football. The game ended 4-0 and Trevor was named in the press as the Man of the Match, scoring two goals. The local press were frustrated. They wanted, like many Villa fans, to see him out there playing his exciting game; they always made comment regarding what Villa could do with a fully fit Ford. But injury was part and parcel of his game. There were no top physios in those days and playing the type of game Trevor did, like many centre forwards of the day, they were always going to get hurt and miss games. The Welshman continued to turn it on for the home fans as he netted two in a 3-3 draw with Grimsby Town. Trevor again missed the next couple of games but returned in May to face both Blackburn Rovers and Preston North End at home, winning both games. Villa ended the season in eighth position as Liverpool won the league. For Trevor, he had played nine games and scored nine goals, making him the club's third-highest goal-scorer of the season, behind George Edwards on ten and Dickie Dorsett on thirteen – not bad considering he had only joined in January. However, for Trevor and his own high standards meant he wanted to be top dog and third place was just not good enough. He had also established himself with the fans and he thought it was quite strange that he had none of the abuse from the terraces for his style of play that he had received at the Vetch.

With the summer in full swing, Trevor returned to Swansea to see his family and concentrate on his cricket, where he was a regular for a Glamorgan eleven who played mainly one-day and friendlies as opposed to county cricket. Trevor loved the game and was a very highly thought of fast-bowler and batsman, and he always thought of cricket as a way to get away from football but keep his competitive edge. Returning to Swansea, he was just Trevor. The people at Townhill always asked how he was getting on, but there was certainly no star treatment for him and he certainly never expected any from them. His return to Swansea did however make a perfect opportunity for some supporters to tell him what they thought of him in relation to of Swansea's decline since he left. The goals dried up for the

Swans without Trevor there and it appeared the side became low in confidence after their relegation. Players like Ernie Jones and Frankie Squires were also sold by order of the board, and this went against Haydn Green's philosophy, so he decided to step aside and leave the club. Green managed Watford for one season in the early 1950s and then left the game altogether. He passed away, aged seventy-four, in 1957. It was a sad loss to football as Green was certainly ahead of his time in terms of footballing philosophy; his vision of developing young talent was picked up by the likes of Stan Cullis at Wolves and Matt Busby at Manchester United years later, and it proved to be very successful. Trevor was called a rat by some sections of the crowd as they thought he had left a sinking ship. They also accused him of being a big head as he 'swanned' around the town with his 'posh clothes and money'. Trevor remembered how those very supporters said he would never make the grade. The stinging accusations hurt him deeply as he loved the town and the club, but he realized it was only a minority of Swansea supporters who felt this way and it also brought home the fact that he had done the right thing in moving away.

The 1947/48 season could not come quick enough for Trevor, and he felt he could really do something in the forthcoming months. Villa started the season in an inconsistent mood, losing their opening game 3-0 away at Grimsby Town following the defeat with two draws away at Sunderland and home to Manchester City. The club's first win was a 2-0 victory over Sunderland in front of the Villa faithful. Trevor was named Man of the Match by the local paper, referring to him as 'Like a constant battering ram smashing down the Sunderland defence with every chance he got.' As the season progressed it was obvious that Villa were not going to be pulling up any trees that season but for Trevor it was certainly one where he found his feet at the club. Still with the constant threat of injury his reputation throughout football was growing at an incredible pace. As the year ended, Villa were just outside the top ten and the man from Swansea had scored ten goals in twenty-two games. He felt that he was on his way to becoming a top player.

One game in particular that stood out during this time was the FA Cup third round tie against Manchester United at a rain-soaked Villa Park. A crowd of 65,000 packed into the ground and it was a game that Trevor remembered as the best game he had ever played in while at Villa. The teams' line-ups were as follows:

Aston Villa – Jones, Potts, Parkes, Dorsett, Moss, Lowe, Edwards, Martin, Ford, Brown, Smith.

Manchester United – Crompton, Carey, Aston, Anderson, Chilton, Cockburn, Delaney, Morris, Rowley, Pearson, Mitten.

United were certainly the favourites going into the game, but Villa were in an upbeat mood. Within seconds of the whistle, Villa kicked off and Trevor pushed the ball into teammate Brown who then put a pinpoint ball out to Smith. His cross was met by George Edwards and Villa found themselves 1-0 up, with Villa Park in raptures. This start certainly brought a very good United side into life under the orchestration of captain Johnny Carey. Within five minutes United were brought level by Jack Rowley after some excellent work from winger Charlie Mitten. United went from strength to strength and built up a 5-1 lead with Villa not even getting anywhere near the ball. The inquest at half-time led the team to go for it during the second half, but as Villa kept going they were rewarded with three goals and a score line of 5-4 with ten minutes to go. The whole of Villa Park was on its feet as the home team pressed and pressed to get level. Incredibly more goals were to come. Trevor summoned every effort to strike the ball from outside the box, but it was heartbreak as he saw it strike the bar and fall away. All the players were dead on their feet as United had a last gasp corner that United forward Pearson headed into the net to make it 6-4. As the two teams trudged off the field United players shook Trevor's hand and thanked him for the tough game and the fight back. It was a wonderful game at the very top of British football and although Villa had lost and Trevor had not found the net he was not bothered on this occasion as he knew he was up there with the best in the game. The match stayed with Villa fans and Trevor; in later life he referred to it as the match where he felt most comfortable with the game's elite.

The season continued to bring inconsistency to the club, although the team rallied towards the end of the year to finish a respectable sixth behind eventual champions, Arsenal. Trevor was top goalscorer with eighteen goals, and this stat boosted his confidence in the dressing room.

With the summer over, the 1948/49 season started for Villa with a 2-1 win at home against Liverpool. It also meant two goals for Trevor, both with his head from corners. There was the usual altercation with defenders and rival 'keeper who thought he was going in too hard, but to the 36,000 at Villa Park he was fast becoming a hero to the club. Unfortunately, after the win the club hit terrible form and lost six of their next eight matches. The press started to talk about the possibility of relegation. Trevor also hit a barren run and after training he told manager Massie that he thought the team should get the ball up to him quicker. This was not some player throwing his toys out of the pram. Trevor had thought this from the moment he signed, but did not want to rock the boat. However, due to defeat after defeat he felt he had to make his feelings known as the style of play was starting to affect his goalscoring chances. Often he would find himself with two centre-backs on him and winning the ball was becoming an issue. He and the players spoke at length about what their problems were, but it was only Trevor who spoke out even though they were all thinking it. In the back of his mind he thought the other players' silence had all the hallmarks of what had happened at Swansea when he refused to stay in the retreat. Manager Massie told him that he would take on board what he said, but as far as Trevor was concerned, that reply was as good as a no.

The club's poor run also fired the board into action and they decided, as they had done in previous seasons, to spend their way out of the slump. They brought in Welsh wing-half Ivor Powell from QPR, Colin Gibson, an inside right from Newcastle United, and utility player Con Martin from Leeds United. Martin was one of those strange breeds that could play defender and goalkeeper, and do both tasks admirably. He would later become a fans' favourite at Villa Park. In total the board had spent £50,000 on the trio. Things picked up for a while with the club posting some memorable wins, notably a 5-1 victory against neighbours Wolverhampton Wanderers with Trevor netting four goals in the game. In fact, the local paper referred to his performance as 'Herculean', which was a term that had never been applied to Trevor before. He loved it (when he had worked out what it meant). The club again suffered from inconsistency and the win against Wolves was followed by a dismal 5-2 home defeat against Blackpool that led to some hostile booing from the Villa Park faithful after the game. Manager Alex Massie called an emergency meeting with his players at the training ground. As the team arrived they were full of speculation as to what they might hear. With them all present, Alex Massie produced a large blackboard and explained that he was going to make a few tactical changes. Firstly, and most significantly, he wanted Villa to take on a more direct style of play that would make better use of Trevor – in other words get the ball out wide quickly and get crosses in or get it up quickly for him to fight and win the ball one on one with defenders. With Trevor's speed and aggression, the plan was that he would win the ball and bring in others to play if he did not have a chance himself. Massie was also moving Ivor Powell in the back line along with Frank Moss as he felt they would complement each other more. The news thrilled Trevor as he felt like Massie was building the team around him. As the players filled out of the dressing room, Massie caught hold of Trevor and pulled him aside. 'It's up to you now Trevor', he smiled. The revival was dramatic as Villa lost only one of their remaining seventeen games, finishing in tenth position, with Portsmouth winning the league. As for Trevor, again he was top goal-scorer at the club with fourteen goals in thirty-five games. His goal return was not as much as the previous season, but he felt that the clubs were fitting around him, which in turn was rapidly making him top dog at the club. And that was something Trevor strived for no matter where or who he was playing for.

5

Knowing Your Worth

It is well documented that Trevor Ford was a man who loved the good things in life. Always immaculately dressed and with a mop of jet-black hair, he looked every inch the Hollywood star; in fact, when his career ended he was contacted by an agent based at Pinewood Studios, London, and offered the chance to move into acting, but Trevor knew it was not his thing and declined the offer with a smile. As Trevor's popularity grew, more and more people wanted to know him, especially members of the opposite sex. But there was only one girl for Trevor, and that was Louise Morgan, who later became Louise Ford.

Trevor first became aware of Louise in 1942 when, as a youngster with Swansea Town, he and his teammates frequented the Red Cow public house that just so happened to be owned by a certain Mr Morgan, Louise's father. It was well known through Trevor's Swansea teammates that he had a bit of a soft spot for the landlord's dark-haired daughter. Now Trevor was never really a drinker, and he would make his one pint last as long as he could so he could at least stare at her across the bar. He had, up to this point, never actually spoken to Louise, so his teammates bet him five bob to go into the bar on his own, order a pint and, more importantly, ask her out. Although surprisingly shy, Trevor plucked up the courage and walked into the bar. This was certainly an incident that was not motivated by the money and it went against the reputation Trevor would have throughout his career. He stammered out his order and quickly asked if she would accompany him to the cinema the forthcoming Saturday. His face said it all as he walked out of the Red Cow. He asked his mates where the five bob was. With that they all laughed and patted him on the back.

Trevor and Louise went out for a few weeks before Trevor was called up to the Army. While he was away they wrote to each other, but the letters became fewer and fewer and eventually the relationship fizzled out. Trevor, who was never short of female attention, went out with various members of the opposite sex. Young Trevor became serious with one local girl called Doris, and they dated regularly, with Trevor seeing her throughout his early football and Army career. Doris had known Trevor since school and they seemed happy together. The young couple decided to get married and by now Doris and her family had moved to London. The young couple married in Finsbury Park in 1944. Trevor was twenty-one years old. The couple moved back to Swansea and got a flat close to Trevor's parents. The pressure on their relationship grew and grew as Trevor was away with the Army and Swansea Town, leaving young Doris alone. Although Trevor's mother helped, she was constantly missing her own family and the pressure on the couple increased when they had a son, Thomas, a year later. Trevor was thrilled to have a son, but deep down he never really felt that married life was for him. Doris was desperate to move back home, which lead to arguments between them, and unfortunately for the young family Trevor and Doris were divorced months after Thomas was born. Doris took Thomas back to London. The pair met up regularly so Trevor could still have contact with Thomas, but after a few months the visits became less frequent, much to Trevor's shame, and eventually all contact was lost. Professionally his career went from strength to strength, but privately the whole episode had scarred him. He realized that he never really loved Doris and he felt massive guilt towards not being a father to Thomas. In reflection, his thoughts always came back to Louise and what she was doing now. Was she the one that got away?

Fast forward a couple of years and the young Trevor arrived in Swansea on leave from the Army. He caught a bus from the High Street station to Townhill. The bus was packed, so he went upstairs. There was only one remaining seat, and that was next to a young women who just happened to be Louise. They got chatting and Louise told Trevor that her father had passed away and that she was now seeing a young man who was an accountant. Trevor's son David takes up the story:

> The meeting had a great effect on Dad. I don't think he ever forgot Mum, and although they were not long on the bus the flame between them was still there. Dad always told us that Mum's Mum was not keen on her daughter being with a footballer. She also thought that the accountant had better prospects, which seems laughable today when you think of how some girls aspire to be WAGS. Anyway, Dad won her over and Mum dumped the other lad. They married at St Paul's Congregational Church in Swansea in 1948 whilst Dad was at Aston Villa. He was living in a flat up there, but the club arranged for him to move into a large three-bedroom house in the Handsworth area of Birmingham. The house was fitted with every conceivable mod con of the day, like a washing machine and fridge, and in some ways these gifts from the club were a way of looking after players and their families back then.

The 1949/50 season started with a draw for Villa away at Manchester City. The newly married Ford hit the ground running, with four goals in the opening five games, as he continued to forge a reputation as one of the hardest and most exciting centre forwards in the country. As the season progressed, Villa found themselves mid-table. Trevor was happy with his nine goals in fifteen games tally. With Christmas on the horizon, Villa played rivals Birmingham City at Villa Park. The game was an intense affair and it pitched Trevor against Birmingham and England 'keeper Gil Merrick. There was certainly no love lost between these two as they had locked horns over the years, and Trevor always seemed to score against Merrick. Football then was a very different animal in terms of contact. Nowadays 'keepers can't be touched and all decisions go the way of the 'keeper, but back in the 1940s and 1950s keepers were fair game and the shoulder charge was legal. Yes, the football purists didn't always accept it, but it was part of the game. 'Keepers were also known to take a handful of sand from the pitch before a corner and fling it into the centre forward's eyes as he came to attack the ball. As far as Gil Merrick was concerned, Ford's rough attacking style had no place in the game, and in 1954 Merrick would release a book called *I See It All* in which he described his time in football along with certain tips for young 'keepers. One chapter in the book is called 'players in the game' and refers to different forwards he had played against. He described Ford as:

> A menace to a goalkeeper's reputation. He is always chasing the keeper and never gives him a moments rest. He can hit a ball extremely hard and to dive at his feet is a desperate business. He is most dangerous of all when he comes in for the keeper off his feet and at full stretch, grasping for a high ball.

Reading the quote nowadays, many would think it was a pretty good description of the Welshman, but Trevor took exception to the thought that he was dangerous to 'keepers and sued Merrick in the courts, winning the case and £250 damages. Merrick later revealed that he only made around £250 from the book anyway. Looking back on the incident it seems that Trevor knew there was more to his game than just roughing up the opposing 'keeper – after all he had never been sent off or booked in his career – and maybe he felt that he was not given the credit he felt he should've received.

True to form, Trevor scored for Villa in a 1-1 draw against their rivals in yet another tense affair. Louise had become pregnant and was due to give birth in the summer. The happy couple were overjoyed at the news and decided that Louise should go back to her mother in Swansea as the due date drew nearer. Trevor would continue living in Birmingham and would travel back to Wales whenever he could. This season was another one of inconsistency for the club. Trevor was starting to miss more games due to his style of play, opposing defenders who were doing everything in their power to stop him, both legally and illegally. The season drifted along and the club was knocked out of the FA Cup after three attempts by Middlesbrough. There was another game against rivals Birmingham, with Trevor netting both goals in a 2-2 draw. The club also suffered two bad defeats by Manchester United – 4-0 at home and a 7-0 hammering at Old Trafford. Villa finished the season in a disappointing twelfth place. Trevor again was the top scorer with eighteen goals in thirty-nine league and cup appearances.

Just before the end of the season, Trevor received a phone call that could have changed his life forever. The call came from Jack Dodds, an ex-professional who had played for Everton and Scotland. Dodds was now the representative for Colombian side Millonarios. Football back in Trevor's time was a completely different industry to the one we see today – players earning fortunes that the average man in the street can only dream about. Back then Trevor was on £10 per week during the season and £7 during the summer; even though he was Villa's costliest player, he would have received the same as any run-of-the-mill player at the club, the only difference being his £10 signing-on fee from a transfer. Compare that with Aston Villa who were averaging gates at around 40,000 and charging fans two bob (10p), which equated to £4,000 per fortnight to the club, and their wage bill for forty professionals was around £400 a week. It was plain to see that clubs were making good money while players' wages were set in stone. This was common practice throughout the game. Compared to the average factory worker, who was earning £6 a week at the time, players' wages were not that bad, but the problem lay in the fact that they had no control over their own destiny. One incredible fact that shows the lack of pay and respect to footballers of the past was that in FA Cup finals, which regularly pulled in crowds of 100,000, the winning players were restricted to bonuses of £20 each and the losers received nothing. The marching band that played at half-time received £350, which was £80 more than the winning team. This injustice towards footballers gave rise to many of the top stars such as Stoke City and England defender Neil Franklin, Manchester United and England winger Charlie Mitten, Swansea Town and Wales defender Roy Paul, Stoke City winger George Mountford, Bobby Flanell and Billy Higgins from Heart of Midlothian, Jack Hedley from Everton and, of course, Trevor Ford being contacted by agents representing Colombian Football League clubs such as Santa FE and Millonarios. At the time these South American clubs could pay what they wanted as they were not under the jurisdiction of UEFA. Trevor was very interested, especially as in a few weeks he would become a father. Millonarios were offering him a £3,000 signing-on fee, and £35 a week. They would also provide him and Louise with a fully furnished apartment, a new sports car and flights back and forth to the UK a couple of times a year. There was also the added bonus of Trevor playing twenty-eight games a season instead of forty-two, and also the opportunity to negotiate the length of his own contract, which was something far removed from the 'take it or leave it' attitude of UK clubs. Trevor agreed in principle, but told them he would be out in a few weeks. Franklin, Mitten, Paul, Flannel, Higgins, Hedley and Mountford all flew off to South America, leaving football in turmoil back home as news of these fantastic offers spread like wildfire throughout the game and the press. Trevor, being Trevor, thought long and hard about the deal. He knew that it was a momentous step for him and his family and he was very flattered that he had come to the attention of the Colombians. There was part of him that thought maybe friend and ex-teammate Roy Paul had something to do with that. He knew he would have to talk things over with Louise and there was much to consider, in particular the small matter of walking out on Aston Villa and basically doing a midnight flit like the other players had. Before going back to Wales he went back to Villa Park and had a look around for what he thought would be his last time. The club had been good to him on and off the field, and he knew that it wasn't right just to leave without any sort of explanation. He knew if Villa got wind of it they would not cancel his contract and allow him to go, but this deal could set him up for life. He also felt frustrated, like many other top footballers, regarding the way in which the clubs seemed to own you. He knew what he was worth and that the Villa public paid their money to see him perform on the pitch, for which he received a straight £10 – the same as a lad who had just signed professional forms. One of the players who headed for Bogota was Charlie Mitten and he explained in his excellent book *Bogota Bandit* how the players were feeling:

> These days we take millionaire footballers for granted. Today any Manchester United player could buy a new family car for cash. In 1950 none could ever dream about doing that with a second-hand banger, even though a new car cost £100. We were aware that we were making large amounts of money for clubs, and although we were not poor it wasn't right. I agreed and this was whilst I was on a tour of America with United. I then decided I had to go and tell Matt Busby the news. I knocked on his door to tell him and he was very angry. 'You can't do that', he

said. 'You're not allowed.' 'I am,' I explained, as my contract had run out. 'That does not matter, we own the contract and we have decided to resign you next season,' he replied. I told him I was twenty-nine years old and I wanted to make some real money, and with that he quieted down as I told him the offer. 'They don't want a manager as well do they? Charlie you better go or you will die wondering,' he replied.

The players were lambasted by some of the football authorities and the Players' Union made no comment on the defection. English football's golden boy at the time, Billy Wright, came out and said that footballers should be happy with their pay. Many in the Professional Footballers Association found those comments unhelpful as the defection could spark a change in the game and open up debate into the way players were treated. Trevor packed his bag and left for Wales, stopping off at the *Western Mail* offices in Cardiff to see if there was any word from the lads, in particular from Roy Paul. When he got to the newspaper's offices there was no news, so he continued on his journey to Swansea. There he talked it over with Louise and their families, and although they knew it would be hard, the families gave their blessing. That night Trevor received a call from a journalist friend who told him that Roy and many of the lads were coming home and it would be in tomorrow's paper. At the first sight of light Trevor ran down to the shop. On the back pages was news that Roy Paul and Jack Hedley were indeed coming home. Roy then contacted Trevor and said 'Don't think about going.' Apparently thirty-six hours after arriving, the Millonarios club treated them like film stars with flags and waving fans, but after a while there was a reluctance to come up with the offers and the players duly came home. Mitten, Mountford, Flavell and Franklin stayed and enjoyed their time in Colombia, but when they returned the football authorities shunned them. All were suspended and their clubs sold them all. They also found their international careers over, something that was particularly hard on Franklin, who at the time was England's best defender. Mitten said later:

I like that some of the other lads were held up before the Football Association like naughty boys. The twelve men in blazers wanted to know what money we were on, all about our contracts, and I told them it was none of their business. They were not interested in whether there was any danger of a South American side beating England in years to come or what the coaching was like, or how the game was run. No it was about punishing us. Then I remember they said to me 'Do you know you have forced Manchester United to transfer you?' Forced them? I thought it must be very painful for United being forced to transfer me for only £22,000. And out of that I received my original 1938 £20 signing-on fee.

The whole incident started a change in football, which admittedly would come some years later, but it forced the Professional Footballers Association to become bigger and start representing its members in a more aggressive way.

As for Trevor, he thanked his lucky stars that he had delayed the venture, but it certainly got him thinking about his future security in the game, particularly as he was now a father to newborn son David. He made a promise to himself that he was going to get it right and not let David down like he had with Thomas. The time Louise had spent in Swansea made her homesick for Wales and this uncertainty was all around the house at the start of the 1950/51 season. This also coincided with a massive family problem that had developed back home. Trevor's father had left his mother Daisy for a local girl called Carol. Carol had in fact been a former girlfriend of Trevor's and there was an age gap between Carol and Trevor's father of thirty years. The couple had now moved to London and Trevor raced home to Swansea to console his mother and his other siblings, Ivor, Ronald and Joan. There was no contact with Trevor's father and as far as young Trevor was concerned, that was the end of the matter. He struggled to come to terms with his father's actions.

After this terrible event Trevor was glad to get back to football. He made sure that nobody would know what had happened in his private life. Villa started the season well with a 2-0 victory over neighbours WBA at Villa Park and a 3-1 win again at home to Sunderland, but the club then went nine games without a win. Trevor's goal-scoring touch had deserted him with only one goal to show for his efforts. He became more and more frustrated and things did not get easier when manager Alex Massie was sacked and replaced by former Newcastle United boss George Martin. Trevor liked Massie, and although he was happy for Martin to be in the boss's chair, things just did not feel the same at the club. Martin was another Scot who, as a player, had won the league with Everton in 1928. He had been manager of Newcastle United and was certainly not afraid of making unpopular decisions, like selling Newcastle star player Len Shackleton to rivals Sunderland for £20,000. Fans were very upset but Martin's judgment was proved right when Newcastle went on to win promotion. Back on the pitch, Trevor hit the net for only the second time away against Huddersfield in a 4-2 defeat. The game would prove to be his last in the claret and blue of Villa. With unrest at home, Trevor decided that it might help him on and off the field if he moved to another club. He decided to meet secretary Billy Smith and told him that he wanted a transfer. With that, the transfer wheels went into overdrive and within a matter of hours clubs were expressing an interest in signing the Welsh centre forward. Mr Fred Normansell, the Villa chairman, called him into his boardroom and told Trevor that the club's interests were Swansea Town, Cardiff City, Chelsea and Sunderland. He also told Trevor that it was up to him as the club did not want him to leave as they felt he had been a great servant to Aston Villa.

During next few days Trevor talked to all the clubs. He entered into the discussions more than happy to ask each representative what they could do for him. Villa had looked after him, and if the clubs wanted him they had to show him how much. It was obvious that he still had the Colombian incident fresh in his mind. He firstly spoke with Swansea Town chairman Abe Freeman who told him they were very interested, but Trevor knew in his heart of hearts it would be a backward step for him to drop a division and join the Swans again. He was upfront with Freeman and he understood. Next was Cardiff City manager Cyril Spiers who played on the fact that he would be coming home to Wales, and what a benefit it would be to his home life. Trevor told Spiers that he would give him his answer after he had spoken to Sunderland and Chelsea. Trevor liked Chelsea manager Billy Birrell, and he told Trevor that surely every player would like to play in London and how great it would be for his wife with all the shopping on offer. Trevor thought long and hard and then asked him, 'What else is in it for me?' Birrell never flinched and said a house would be available and a job outside of football worth around £750 a year. Again he told him that he would give his decision after speaking to Sunderland. Bill Murray, the Sunderland manager, was next up. He and Trevor hit it off immediately. Murray was full of enthusiasm and determination to sell the club to Trevor. He told him that he would have a terrific future at the club, where money was no object, and they prided themselves in looking after players and their families. He told Trevor that a job at a motor firm was lined up for him worth £1,000 a year, and if he succeeded at that then he would be a director of the firm. He also told Trevor to choose a house and the club would buy it and have it decorated to his wife's requirements. Trevor talked things over with Louise, and although she still had yearnings for south Wales, she backed what he felt in his heart was right in terms of football and security for his young family – and that was Sunderland.

He told the other chairmen of his decision and they were all far from happy. At this time he still had no idea what the fee would be. On the afternoon of 27 October 1950 the lad from Townhill, Swansea, became the world's costliest footballer with a £30,000 fee on his head; the previous record had been £26,500, paid by Preston North End for the services of Sheffield Wednesday's inside forward Eddie Quigley the previous year. With the press happy with their stories, and everything signed, he went back to Aston Villa to say goodbye. Aston Villa and England inside forward Tommy Thompson remembered it well:

> I was gutted when Trevor left. Manager George Martin brought me to the club from Newcastle United as a way of helping Trevor get goals. I remember when I joined, he was a smashing bloke. He would help anybody and he was a real star in the dressing room, but you never felt he was a big-head. He was a great trainer and was so strong. I remember playing against him in a practice match and he frequently charged me off the ball with his strength. When he left, he went round all of us and shook our hands. We all gave him some stick about being the costliest player but he took it in good part. It's a real regret for me that I never got to play a couple of seasons with him. It was certainly Villa's loss.

Trevor was so excited to be joining a club the size of Sunderland. He couldn't wait to get started and wear the red and white stripes, playing alongside such greats as Len Shackleton and Ivor Broadis, who would be his striking partners.

The newspapers were full of news regarding the Trevor Ford transfer both nationally and in his home country of Wales although not all of it was positive. Many of the Welsh fans of Swansea and Cardiff were not happy that a Welshman had snubbed a Welsh club. Chelsea also had their nose put out of joint that he did not want to sign for a London club or live in the capital. Trevor just dismissed it as paper talk but little did he know this story had not been put to bed by any means.

6

The Bank of England Club

Sunderland Football Club have always been a massive club, and in 1950 they were possibly the biggest. Although formed in 1879, they were not in the original football league of 1888 until three years after its formation. This was due to geographical issues: the main bulk of teams in the league were from the Midlands and the North West. Sunderland were always knocking on the door, and although Preston North End won the first league title in 1888, and Aston Villa one year later, both of them were beaten by Sunderland in friendlies. These results showed how clearly the side from the North East had to be elected to the league, and in 1890 the Football Association agreed on the promise that Sunderland would pay the travelling teams' expenses due to their position on the map. There in started a rich tradition with the club winning six league titles, their last one being in 1936.

The club that Trevor signed for was watched over by chairman Edward Ditchburn, a local businessman who made his money as a furniture manufacturer. He had also been mayor of Sunderland in the 1930s. Manager was Bill Murray, with whom Trevor had his negotiations. Murray had played right-back for the club in the 1930s and was part of the league-winning side of 1936, returning to take over the club in 1939. His first real signing was Len Shackleton from Newcastle United for a record £20,000 in 1948. This caused a real excitement around the club and a new league attendance was set in the April when 61,084 packed into Roker Park to watch a game against Blackpool. Prior to Trevor's arrival, the club had splashed out on Ivor Broadis from Carlisle

United, paying £18,000 for the inside forward, and Tommy Wright, a winger from Partick Thistle who cost £12,000. The new signings paid off and the club became the highest scorers in the First Division for the 1949/50 season, twenty-five of the goals coming from their centre forward, Dickie Davis.

Unfortunately for the club, they finished the season in third place; they would have won the league title except for a dreadful defeat at home on the last day to Manchester City in a game where they missed two penalties.

Ditchburn and the Sunderland board's answer to that gut-wrenching loss of the title was to get the chequebook out and keep spending. Trevor arrived along with Northern Ireland winger Billy Bingham, who signed from Irish side Glentoran for £10,000 as the club pushed for their first title since 1936. Billy said of the move,

> It was massive for me to go to a club like Sunderland and it helped me coming in at the same time as Trevor as all the emphasis was on him, what with the big fee. He was brilliant to me and he helped me in many ways with my game. What struck me about him was that he was a very quiet man off the pitch, and although he was a huge star, he was incredibly modest and I think that's why the lads took to him so well.

After all the euphoria of Trevor's arrival, Murray put him straight into the side to play Chelsea at Stamford Bridge, the number nine on his back.

Trevor and Bill Murray caught the train from Birmingham down to London, where Trevor would be introduced to his Sunderland teammates at their hotel before the Chelsea game. All the players were sat in a private lounge and Trevor was introduced to them one by one. Shackleton was injured but still came down to London with the side. It was Trevor's first real meeting with him and they again shook hands, with Shackleton wishing him well. With Trevor all set to play against Chelsea, there was suddenly a last-minute problem with the transfer. Murray received a call from Sunderland secretary Mr Crow who told the Sunderland manager that he had just spoken to Mr Howarth, the Football League secretary, to check that the paperwork had been received at the headquarters in Preston.

Howarth informed him that Aston Villa secretary Mr Smith had not signed Villa's part of the deal, meaning there was a chance that Trevor could not make his debut. However, Howarth said he would see what they could do. Murray and Trevor had a long wait at the hotel; many of the players had already gone to bed. Then late into the evening Crow phoned the hotel reception and the pair were told that Howarth saw it as a technical oversight and allowed it to go through. When the team arrived at Stamford Bridge it seemed the whole of the British press were camped outside waiting for the new record signing. The team ran out and all eyes were on Trevor. Sunderland were well beaten 3-0, and as for Trevor, he hardly had a kick. Whether it was the price tag or the will to prove he was worth the money, he felt sick with his display. It was no comfort that the whole of the team had played badly. As the team got dressed and ready for the train home, his only comfort, apart from going back to the arms of Louise, was the thought that at least it was not in front of those Sunderland fans at Roker Park.

Trevor's home debut could not come quick enough. There were 49,000 people packed into Roker Park for the arrival of Sheffield Wednesday. As the teams waited in the tunnel, photographers flashed their cameras at Trevor. The chaos was lifted when the teams ran onto the pitch and a huge roar went up when the fans saw the men in red and white. Trevor found himself up front alongside Len Shackleton at number ten and Dickie Davis, last season's leading scorer moving to number eight. Trevor knew that this was his chance to make an impact on those fans. He had always done well against them when he played for Aston Villa, so they knew what he was all about, but this time it was his chance to do it in the red and white stripes of Sunderland. As the whistle blew, Trevor spat on his hands and took off in chase of the ball. It was Trevor's first taste of Len Shackleton, whom all the Sunderland play revolved around. Shackleton put Sunderland 1-0 up after a header that left Wednesday 'keeper McIntosh no chance. Then Tommy Wright put the Roker men 2-0 before Sheffield Wednesday pulled one back just before the break. Trevor became more and more frustrated as he found himself in good positions, but the ball never came. In his book *I Lead the Attack*, Trevor explains his frustration over Shackleton: 'I could not make head nor tail of him. A pass would go out to him and I would run into open space ready to receive, but my efforts were wasted. The ball never came my way from him.' Then Shackleton pulled off a stroke of genius and in the second half he sent a perfect cross over to Trevor, who buried the ball into the net with a fine header. Trevor had been battling hard against Sheffield Wednesday centre half Edgar Packard, who in fairness was giving as good as he got, when suddenly a ball was pumped up front. Trevor threw himself towards the ball just as Packard went up for it, resulting in a clash of heads that left the Wednesday centre half with a broken jaw. Minutes later Trevor picked up a ball and crashed it into the net to put the Roker men 4-1 up. As the crowd went delirious the Welshman was still not finished, and in the dying minutes he crashed into McIntosh in the Wednesday goal, sending the 'keeper and the ball into the back of the net. This not only got his hat-trick, but the force of the challenge snapped one of the goal posts at the base. What an introduction to the Roker crowd! He had scored a hat-trick, broke a centre half's jaw and a goal post. The game enhanced Trevor's fearsome reputation throughout football, although Argos, who wrote for the *Sunderland Echo* and was never one for over-the-top praise, gave a different slant on the Welshman's epic game. He wrote,

> Looking back over Sunderland's 5-1 victory, I am not so much concerned with Ford's hat-trick as I am with him fitting in with the rest of the side. Ford got the type of service he required and don't forget he had no practice with his new colleagues, in fact his only practice had been playing his two games. It was unfortunately that Shackleton came off when the game was already won but there is great promise, especially when we get Broadis back from injury.

Trevor was the toast of the side after the game. He also felt in that one match that he could play with the best and be ranked as one of the best. In football terms there won't be many better home debuts than Trevor's at Sunderland.

Trevor and his family was put up in a city hotel before being moved to a house of their choice. Trevor's life started to settle down and he and his family felt at home in the North East. The family moved into a lovely three-bedroom house in the Whitburn area of Sunderland where other players lived, and the families became close, which helped Louise and the young David. The house cost them 30 shillings in rent, which was well below the going rate on rentals of that kind of property. As a couple they were also invited to many gala dinners and charity events across the North East. They were even invited down to London to visit Pinewood Studios – while there they were allowed onto the set to meet comedian Norman Wisdom who was filming his latest film, *Trouble in Store*. Invitations to events and autograph hunters wherever they went made the couple realize that Trevor was big business now, and people were not only interested in the footballer but his wife as well. Trevor was introduced to club director William Martin, who would later become a good friend to Trevor. Martin owned around twenty garages in the area and it was at one of these that Trevor would work selling cars. He was initially just going to be used as a sales tool. Trevor enjoyed the work and he became very popular at the various dealerships. He would sell cars such as Rovers, Fords, Jaguars and the occasional Mercedes Benz. He enjoyed meeting people, especially when the chat got around to football. Martin was very much a self-made man and he liked Trevor's ability to speak to all sorts of people. He would always ask how Trevor and the family were and if they needed anything. They socialized together and he was always Trevor's voice in the boardroom. Martin would arrange for the two of them to meet for lunch and a game of snooker now and then. Trevor was certainly no fantastic snooker player but he was alright, yet Martin would bet Trevor £100 a game. At first Trevor was mortified at the thought of losing that amount of money, but Martin assured him it would be fine. Martin lost every time they played and soon Trevor realized that it was the club's way of 'looking after him and his family'.

Although Trevor was settled at the club, tongues started wagging and rumours started to circulate throughout the football world regarding his transfer from Aston Villa. People were saying that Trevor had told all the clubs interested in him that he had wanted a large cash payment before signing. When the rumours became intolerable, Trevor was called into manager Murray's office. Murray told Trevor not to worry, but the Football League had decided to look into the transfer and there would be an inquiry. The two men were called down to face the Football League management committee in London, as Trevor was being charged by Rule 67 that stated 'Any Player may not request excess of the £10 signing-on fee from the purchasing club.' Trevor was called into a large oak-panelled room with seven officials led by Arthur Drewry. Drewry was a director of Grimsby Town who had made his money in the fishing trade; he also served as a selector for the England team along with around ten other chairman of different football clubs around the country, so it was plain to see the position of power gentleman like Mr Drewry had at this time. He told Trevor that he was alleged to have asked for more than his £10 signing-on fee when he was placed on the open transfer list. He also stated that he had asked for more money than he was entitled to and wanted to know why the Welshman had signed for Sunderland? Trevor replied that the reason he signed for Sunderland was because it would be good for his career to play alongside Shackleton and Broadis. He also told them he was offered a job by the club and it was a chance to win honours there. They listened and took notes. As the interrogation became more and more detailed, Trevor asked to be brought face-to-face with whoever had made these claims, pointing out that it was only their word against his. He also pointed out that there might have been a misunderstanding when he asked about his future security which may have been misinterpreted as a request for a cash payment. The board listened on and told him their final judgment would be in two weeks' time. Trevor left with Murray and the two of them were furious that they had been dragged down to London for this. The fledging Players' Union came out and backed Trevor immediately. Chairman James Guthrie, an ex-player who had played for Dundee and Portsmouth as well as coaching Crystal Palace, spoke to the press regarding the dreadful way that Ford was treated. He said that Trevor had no access to representation from the union and that this case highlighted the fact that a maximum wage should be abolished, along with club ownership of players' contracts. Guthrie was certainly no novice when it came to fighting for players' rights, and he was media savvy with plenty of friends in the press. When he was at Dundee, he led a successful struggle to get summer wages for the players after the club chairman had tried to cut players' wages across the board. He was later sold on to Portsmouth after asking for an unrealistic wage rise from Dundee. While at Portsmouth, he led another campaign to get bonus payments that were owed to the players. The incident, although terrible for Trevor, started to spark the union into a more aggressive approach towards the footballing authorities while also giving the everyday football fan an insight into the players' plight.

Two weeks passed and there was a knock at the family home. Trevor opened the door and was greeted by a reporter from the local paper. 'I have some news for you Mr Ford. You have been fined £100 by the Football Association.' Trevor was livid. He paced around the front room asking who accused him of this. Was it wrong to get the best for yourself and your family? If he had been in any other profession there would be no problem. Trevor felt angry and humiliated. He was annoyed that he was not provided with a written statement of the charges, offered no legal representation, and had no right to hear the evidence against him or permission to reply to the accusations point by point. In that one incident he lost all respect for the football authorities. He did not know who his accusers were and he hoped it had nothing to do with Swansea Town or Cardiff City, after all he had felt a backlash back in Wales when he signed for Aston Villa.

The next morning a London newspaper called and asked him to give his side of the story. They also offered £100 for the interview, so Trevor duly obliged and told the paper of the injustice and the way players were being treated by the authorities. Two days later Trevor received an envelope through the post with £100 in it and a message that read, 'Sorry to hear about your spot of trouble. Perhaps this will help. Good luck on Saturday – exiled Welsh fan.' Trevor was speechless. Although he felt that he had a black mark on him in the eyes of the football authorities, he knew that the man on the terraces was right behind him, and that was all that mattered. Later inquiries over the years found that it was allegedly Chelsea who had accused Trevor of asking for more money. The club had felt aggrieved over his decision to sign for Sunderland instead of the London-based club. What is amazing about the complaint is that when Trevor asked Billy Birrell 'what's in it for me?' the manager never ended the talks or said they could offer nothing as it was against the law. He simply offered Trevor a package to sign just as Sunderland did, yet when they missed out on the signature they went to the powers that be, claiming foul.

The club were inconsistent on the pitch, and although Trevor was doing his share by putting the ball in the net, he found Shackleton frustrating at times to say the least, mainly due to the fact that he could be brilliant in some games and just seem not interested in others, which could also happen during the same game. Trevor found the whole thing very exasperating. The combination of Ford, Shackleton and Broadis just wasn't gelling, and after a few weeks the supporters became fed up. Broadis got the brunt of the fans' anger, which upset Trevor as he had become good friends with the forward. He knew the fans loved Shackleton and Trevor's 'give 100 per cent' attitude, plus that debut meant that he would at least get a bit of time to show what he could do. The local press could see that Trevor was giving his all for the new club. Argos, writing in the *Sunderland Echo* after the club's heavy 5-1 defeat against Arsenal at Highbury, said of Trevor:

> An even worse fact of Sunderland's play was that Trevor Ford was running into open spaces for a pass that never came. He stood where the ball was kicked to him with Leslie Compton on his heels. I reckon he got two good passes in the game. And with such support he was wasted.

Sunderland were dreadfully unpredictable that first season, but the local press were always positive about the £30,000 striker. After a 6-5 defeat to Derby County, the local *Sunderland Echo* singled out Trevor for praise, saying, 'Trevor Ford has never looked so good in a Sunderland shirt. He got a goal with each foot and the Derby keeper did not have a ghost of a chance with any of them.' The club finished the season in a disappointing twelfth place with Trevor finding the net seventeen times, making him the clubs highest scorer for the season, something that the Welshman regarded as his job at whatever club he was playing for. He also felt that this answered any critics he might have had. Straight after the season ended, Sunderland left for a tour of Austria. The club would be away for ten days, basing themselves in Vienna. Going on tour to another country was proof that Trevor was at a massive club; it was a testament to how the club really looked after its pros. As well as the once-a-month snooker game with Mr Martin, but if the club were away in London, taxis would be laid on for the players so they could see one of the latest West End shows. Plus, on the journey back to Sunderland, every player who wanted one could have a packet of cigarettes – something Trevor certainly indulged in. Facilities at the club were second to none, with a state-of-the-art gymnasium and a collection of snooker tables for the players to unwind after training. The clubs were treating players like adults, and what stuck in the throat of Trevor was that the football authorities treated them like children. Everybody got on throughout the tour, although the players were not keen on most of the food. The club laid on sightseeing visits and Trevor spent a fortune on gifts for Louise and young David. Trevor shared a room with Ivor Broadis and the two of them discussed the coming season and hopefully how they and Shackleton could become more of a force up front. They played their first game against Rapid Vienna, going down 5-1 to the Austrian champions. Trevor got the consolation goal, but also fell foul of the Austrian ref who gave him a severe telling off for his aggressive style of play. Another defeat to an Austrian eleven followed; again Trevor scored two of Sunderland's goals in the 5-4 defeat. The trip was finished off by another defeat this time, going down 2-1 to Gratz.

After the tour Trevor would go back to Wales with his family and stay with his mother-in-law. It was a great time to visit family and friends and he always liked signing autographs for local lads who were now in awe of him. He would look after himself by running and playing the odd game of golf, but his great love during the summer was cricket. He spent many days watching Glamorgan cricket club and also played for local sides in and around the area, turning out to be a very handy all-rounder. On his return to the North East he was quickly snapped up by local side Horden cricket club on a summer contract. Although it was local league cricket, Trevor loved it and batted at number six. He also took many wickets as a pace bowler.

When he returned to Sunderland for the 1951/52 season, the club had got the chequebook out again, gaining the services of Scotland international half-back George Aitken from East Fife. The fee was undisclosed, but was thought to be around £16,000. The club also sold Ivor Broadis to Manchester City as they pursued that Championship trophy. Trevor was truly gutted at the Broadis transfer, but was pleased that Ivor had made a success of the move, going on to play for England. He was also pleased that his record of being Britain's most expensive footballer was broken in the March when Sheffield Wednesday paid Notts' County £35,000 for the services of Jackie Sewell. The pressure of the fee had weighed heavy on Trevor's shoulders and now he felt that weight had been lifted. For Sunderland, the season became one of disappointment again as they finished a disappointing twelfth, with Shackleton and Ford sharing the top goalscorer tag within twenty-two each. There was major frustration on the terraces and also in the papers as, in theory, the club had one of the best sides around, but they could not deliver. Fans were also perplexed by the lack of understanding between Shackleton and Ford when they played together, brought home by a 4-1 win at home against Chelsea in the February of the 1951/52 season. During the build-up, Trevor had six teeth removed and it was very much touch and go as to whether he would turn out for the game. The club doctor and the dentist advised him not to, but he passed himself fit for the match. He played and scored a hat-trick, scoring all the goals with his left foot. Shackleton scored to make it 4-0 at half time. The first half the Sunderland team and especially Ford and Shackleton were unplayable on this sort of form. The fans knew they could destroy any side, but with the game already won, it appeared that Shackleton 'switched off' and just went through the motions. Ford was left up front on his own, chasing everything and never giving up as he looked for more goals. This one game highlighted the fact that Shackleton was, without doubt, a genius of a footballer who turned it on when it suited him, yet Trevor was a ninety-minute player who, although never having the same level of skill as Shackleton, never stopped running. Trevor was angry at Shackleton's attitude toward him and the team. Rightly or wrongly, he inflamed the situation by going to his friends at the press, claiming that Shackleton deliberately never passed to him in games. Nothing was done regarding the situation as far as the club were concerned, and Shackleton said nothing except during an end-of-season tour of Holland in a friendly with the Dutch B team, a game Sunderland won 7-3. Shackleton picked up the ball and took on the whole Dutch defence with a mazy dribble. Then rounding the 'keeper, he squared the ball to Trevor to slot home saying, 'There you go don't say I never pass to you.' It was clear to see this could not go on. Something had to give between the two.

7

Shackleton and the End

It is safe to say that even today Leonard Francis Shackleton is somewhat of a god for Sunderland supporters. T-shirts are available in the Sunderland club shop with his famous quote, 'I've no bias towards Newcastle, I don't care who beats them.' And in the pubs around the ground on match days there will always be a story told among Sunderland fans about this mercurial player, whether it is playing a one-two with the corner flag against Chelsea or watching him hit a ball with the precision of a snooker player to see the ball come back to his feet. Shackleton was a true entertainer and one of England's greats, yet in his career he never won a League Championship, or a FA Cup and it seems an injustice that he only gained five caps for England as it appeared his ball-playing skills were not appreciated – something that has continued with England and the relationship with flair players today.

Born in Bradford in 1922, Shackleton was a natural when it came to ball games. He was a star of England schoolboys and signed amateur forms with his local side, Bradford Park Avenue, where he gained a reputation as a skilful player. At sixteen years of age he caught the eye of Arsenal, and the club duly invited him down to London with a view to signing him. Shackleton was full of confidence in his own ability and knew, given the chance, he could impress, but for weeks he found himself painting the Highbury ground and sweeping terraces. Even at that young age he knew he was good and had the strength of character not to be messed about. Things came to a head one morning when Arsenal manager George Allison walked alongside the pitch at Arsenal with some of the coaches. He saw young Shackleton and his young colleagues. Allison lifted his foot up to where Shackleton was sweeping and asked him to do his shoelace up for him. Shackleton told him to do his own bloody shoelace and walked off. Nothing came of it, but it certainly did not do young Len any good in the long run. Weeks later Allison called him into his office and told Shackleton that the club would be letting him go as they did not think he would make it as a player, and to rub salt into the wound, Allison then told the young Yorkshireman that he would be better looking for work outside of football and suggested the local pit or engineering as a career. The meeting was something that Shackleton never forgot, and years later, whenever he got the chance, he would always turn it on when playing against Arsenal. Although bitterly disappointed, there was a real steel in him to prove people wrong. He went back to Bradford Park Avenue, spending six years with them before signing for Newcastle United for £13,000.

Shackleton hated the whole experience of the transfer system. He openly said in the press that he felt like a piece of meat and he was the last to know in terms of the fee. He was happy to sign for the Magpies, but he had a scant regard for the directors who, as he saw it, were holding some sort of auction for his head. During negotiations, he had asked United what was in it for him, and they replied £500, which was a small fortune. But he never got it and that hardly improved his relationship with his new club. His debut for Newcastle is the stuff of legends: six goals in a 13-0 demolition of Newport County. His impact at the club was sensational, but he would always be a thorn in the side of the directors. He was never afraid to voice an opinion, like the time he and captain Joe Harvey were suspended by the club after they complained that the board had promised them better houses in Newcastle. The club eventually agreed that they had reneged on those promises and the players were reinstated. There is also a tale told in Colin Malam's book *Clown Prince of Soccer? The Len Shackleton Story*, where former Newcastle United striker of the 1970s, Malcolm Macdonald, recalls a story told to him by Joe Harvey:

Newcastle manager at the time was George Martin. He told Shack before an important game against Manchester City that they really needed the points. Martin said, 'If you score a hat-trick you can come off.' It's one of those things that you say joking in the dressing room. Anyway Len scored a hat-trick in the first 20 minutes, putting Newcastle 3-0 up. Then he just walked off. Martin was furious screaming at him, 'What the hell are you doing?' To which Shack replied, 'You said I could come off.' That's how he was; he took people at their word and turned it back on them.

Manchester City, with most of the game to play, beat the ten-man Newcastle 4-3. This incident shows not only his skill and talent but his personality, which was unusual and unconventional. There was plainly no thought for his teammates; he was just proving to manager Martin that he could rise to his challenge. Because of his fraught relationship with the Newcastle board, a decision was made to sell the striker, although there was also a campaign among supporters not to sell him, with many of them writing letters to the local paper in support of him. Shackleton had scored twenty-six goals in his sixty games for the Magpies and there were no fewer than twelve clubs lining up to buy him, including Arsenal, who had bid £20,000, which was a British record. Shack, on the other hand, had his eyes set on one club and one club only, and that was a local rival Sunderland. There was no thought regarding going to the local rivals, only what was best for him. Shackleton signed for £20,050. The additional £50 was the idea of the Sunderland negotiators, who thought that an opening bid of £20,000 would put most clubs off after the rival bidders said they would not go any higher. So in 1948 he left Second Division Newcastle United for First Division Sunderland, where he achieved godlike status.

As far as his England career was concerned, he only made five starts for his country and scored one goal in the process. England manager Walter Winterbottom said at the time, 'Shackleton is a solo merchant who is not a team player. He would try all the fancy stuff when it wasn't needed.'– An interesting insight into why England have never really embraced the maverick player. In 1955 he released a book entitled *Clown Prince of Soccer*. In it, he left a chapter completely blank, calling it 'The Average Director's Knowledge of Football.'

What has become strange about the situation between Trevor Ford and Len Shackleton is that over the years people have stated that they were like chalk and cheese, yet in terms of their lives and thoughts on football, they were very similar; they both were not afraid to ask for the best deal for them and their families and both knew their own worth to football clubs; they knew the injustices that were part of the game and wanted it changed. Both had working-class mining backgrounds, both were married with a young family and in their spare time they were very good cricketers who played to a good standard. All of this common ground seemed to count for nothing as they truly did not like each other. The only loser was Sunderland Football Club. Shack was obviously the peoples' champion with a detest for directors, yet Trevor was well groomed and looked like a film star and always had the ear of many directors and had friends in the press. Many felt that Shackleton was jealous of Trevor, especially with him joining the club as Britain's most expensive player – this may well have led to tensions between them. Everybody at the club knew Shackleton was top dog and that he was certainly a more gifted player, yet Trevor possessed that 'never say die' attitude; he was a player who never gave up on the pitch and always gave 100 per cent – something you couldn't always say for Len. Unfortunately, for Sunderland to achieve their target of winning the league, the two men would have to try and work in harmony with each other, ideally with Shack creating chances for Trevor to finish.

Many people had different theories as to why the two never gelled on the field; for instance, teammate and former Northern Ireland manager Billy Bingham said of the pair:

> Many critics thought Trevor was never a good positional player despite being the most dynamic spearhead in the game at the time. I know He never seemed to know what Shackleton was going to do with the ball and subsequently Trevor believed that Shackleton was ignoring him on the field of play.

Whenever there was criticism aimed at Trevor implying it was his fault, he replied by pointing out that Sunderland's other inside forward, Ivor Broadis, never failed to give him the ball when he could. As the 1952/53 season got underway, the club established their usual inconsistent nature with a win followed by a defeat. Trevor's goalscoring continued despite the lack of service and he ended the year on fifteen goals in a total of twenty appearances. However, the rift with Shackleton was getting wider and wider, with the pair not even speaking to each other. Ford's anger towards Shackleton and his apparent lack of effort on the field as he saw it surfaced in his book *I Lead the attack*. Talking about an FA Cup tie with Scunthorpe in January 1953, Ford explained:

> The little Lincolnshire club had held us to a draw at the first meeting and we travelled to their ground for the replay on the Wednesday night. Once again we were being held 1-1 when I came out of a tackle with my ankle broken. Shackleton never knew the decision I had to make at that time, whether to come off or go through the pain of playing on and not have the ignominy of being beat by the division three minnows? I played on and went onto the wing hobbling about with a broken ankle; I even managed to score the winner. I wondered what he would've done?

The local Sunderland newspaper called Ford's performance 'nothing short of heroic'. Teammate Billy Bingham described Trevor's attitude to the game:

> He was the bravest player I ever played with and nobody could head a ball like Trevor. Although he was around 5ft 10in, he was a perfect 11 stone and an amazing athlete. I really needed building up as I was a scrawny nineteen-year-old, so the two of us would do weights, and I don't think he broke a sweat while I was struggling to lift some of them. We would always have a laugh about it afterwards. He would run through a brick wall right to the end of a game and you always knew you had a chance with Trevor in the side. He would always say to me 'Stick it on the near post or the back post Billy and I will find it.' And he always would. He got some terrible knocks from goalkeepers but he also knew how to dish it out and he never complained to refs. Over the years I have worked with many great players but Trevor was something special.

As the second part of the season evolved, the club seemed to be treading water as they saw the leading pack of clubs getting away from them. In April of that year the press became aware of a bid from Italian club Fiorentina for both Sunderland's Trevor Ford and Bolton Wanderers and England centre forward, Nat Lofthouse. The money the Florence club were offering was £2,000 per year with £35-win bonus, along with a house and a three-year contract. No mention was made as to what the fee would be, but both players were interested. Both Sunderland and Bolton Wanderers refused the bid and would obviously not allow the players to talk to the Italian club's representatives. Trevor was bitterly disappointed and although he acknowledged Sunderland's support for him as part of their future plans, he told friends and colleagues he would have jumped at the chance to try life abroad. The move would have also given him a chance to escape the problems he was having at the club. In January the club had sat top of the league, but an appalling finish to the season, with six draws and six defeats, left them in a disappointing ninth position. There were a few positives in the season, one being the emergence of local youngster Stan Anderson who had turned into a fine attacking wing-half. Stan recalls how supportive Trevor was towards him in his first season and gives a real insight to the friction between the Welshman and Shackleton:

I was only a young kid when I joined the club and it was in the 52/53 season that I got my chance. I was working part time on a building site where I would start work at 7.00 a.m. then go to training at Sunderland at 9.00 a.m., then when training was finished I would go back to work. My part-time job meant that I would arrive at the training ground still in my overalls. I would see Trevor arrive dressed immaculately, as though he was going out for dinner. I was in awe of him and he would always chat and encourage me in my game and I never forgot that, after all he was a really big star at the time. I used to love playing with him, as he was great in the air – quick, strong and brave. It angers me to think that we never won the league or the FA Cup with that side, because we had some fantastic players in it. My job was to win the ball and give it to Shack and he would do the rest. Obviously much has been said about Shack's relationship, or lack of it, with Trevor. Shack had the ability to do anything with a ball and I think there was certainly a bit of jealousy when he looked at Trevor. Trevor was one of the best-looking fellas I have ever seen and was always immaculately dressed. In the changing rooms I would sit next to Shack with Trevor opposite us. Trevor would wind Shack up by combing his hair in the mirror and saying 'God I am good looking', to which Shack would nudge me and say, 'Look at that silly bastard.' It really got to Shack, as he was no oil painting to look at. I think the frustration got to him and the only way he could get back at Fordy was to try and humiliate him on the pitch, and Shack had the ability to do that with a ball. I remember one game, I think it was against Cardiff City, we were 1-0 up and I was playing behind them both. Shack went down the line and beat a couple of players, then rounded the 'keeper. He could plainly see Fordy running in for a goal-scoring chance, but Shack placed the ball just a yard ahead of him knowing there was no way he was going to get it. I just had the feeling he never wanted Trevor to score, which made me really angry; even though I was a young kid it did not seem right. The thing is, Shack could do that with a pass; he was an incredible footballer. But it was a shame that they never got on. I think Trevor would've stayed at Sunderland all his career if they had. I know he and his family were very happy up here. I felt privileged to have played with one of the great centre forwards.

The clubs finished the season on a high with a 4-2 home win against Cardiff City. The win in which Trevor scored two goals showed again what the side were capable of, with Shackleton also finding the net. The team played with flair and skill, and at times the Cardiff players were like statues against the Sunderland team. Trevor finished the season with twenty-four goals from thirty-three games.

A tour of Denmark followed the end of the season, and although Trevor was becoming more and more reluctant to be away from home, the club were undefeated in their three games, winning two and drawing the other. Trevor spent the summer months playing cricket for Horden and visiting the family in Swansea. He, Louise and David would spend hours walking along the beach at the Gower talking about his future and how things would pan out. They were both happy in the North East and had a wonderful lifestyle, so on the face of it everything was great. But Trevor's continuing problems with Sunderland's style of play, and of course Shackleton's humiliation of him on the pitch, continued to worry him. As the 1953/54 season arrived, so did more players, which only added to the club's 'Bank of England' tag. The board spent £61,000 on three international players: Jimmy Cowan, a goalkeeper from Morton; Billy Elliott, an outside half from Burnley; and Welsh international defender Ray Daniel from Arsenal. The £27,000 paid for Daniel was a British record for a defender. Trevor was delighted to see another Swansea boy in the dressing room and the two Welshman socialised on many occasions; in fact they both used to play snooker with director Bill Martin, with the same outcome as usual. Despite the new signings, the club won only one of their opening six games and the unrest was plain to see among directors and fans. However, what Sunderland could achieve was shown in their next home game when, with Ford and Shackleton on top form, they destroyed Arsenal 7-1 with Trevor scoring a hat-trick in the process. The result lit up the 60,000 fans who were at Roker Park to see it. In the dressing room afterwards Ford and Shackleton almost came to blows. There is also an alleged incident that Trevor forced Shackleton's head under the water in the team bath before being pulled off the dazed Shackleton by teammates. Cracks were appearing and it just seemed both men had had enough of each other – after all they had just won 7-1. Trevor could also tell that the dressing room had formed its own pro-Shackleton and pro-Ford cliques. Billy Bingham stated: 'It was really disappointing to see. I got on with both players and they were terrific footballers who at times played teams off the park on their own. It was so sad that they just had this friction with each other.'

With a hostile atmosphere among some of the team, Sunderland travelled to Aston Villa. Villa was a club that Trevor had a great affection for and he was still well thought of there. Again Sunderland had no pattern to their play and were losing 2-0 come the interval. Trevor, feeling he had been let down on many different scoring opportunities, told Shackleton so at half-time. Trevor also informed manager Bill Murray that if this was how it was going to be then he would not play the following week against Portsmouth if Shackleton was in the team, forcing the issue to breaking point. Sunderland eventually lost the game 3-1. Murray left it a couple of days then summoned both players into his office and asked them to shake hands and make up. Trevor flatly refused and was omitted from the game against Portsmouth the following week (a 4-1 defeat) with the club telling the press that he was 'resting due to his current lack of form'.

Realizing this situation was never going to be resolved, Trevor handed in a transfer request to the board. One of the first people to speak to him on the matter was director and friend Bill Martin. Martin told him not to be hasty as he had a good life at the club, bearing in mind that he would not only be leaving Sunderland but the job in car sales, which he was good at and where he was well regarded of among the staff and customers. Trevor told him he would be heartbroken to leave but deep down he knew Shackleton would be going nowhere. Martin told him if he left there would always be a job here for him and he would try to give him some contacts in the motor trade wherever he ended up. In the meantime, the press and fans were voicing their opinions, obviously knowing that the Welshman was not just resting. Argos, in the *Sunderland Echo*, wrote,

> Ford's request for a transfer has created a deep impression with Sunderland fans. Coming on top of his hat-trick against Arsenal, it discounts the possibility of 'Loss of Form' being solely responsible for his request, as the official statement indicates. Basis of this trouble is style not form. He has played for three years in a line that has not made the best use of his abilities, and it is my guess that the acute disappointment he suffered at Villa Park before his former club's supporters was just the last straw.
>
> Reluctantly, because his position in Sunderland has been made particularly attractive with a good job outside football, he feels that his future football career lies elsewhere. Knowing him well, I expect to find his attitude in this matter every bit as determined as his attitude to football itself. For all the Sunderland supporters who wish for a change of mind, I can offer little hope.

Fans also wrote into the paper on hearing the news of Trevor's transfer request:

> I have been a Sunderland supporter for a number of years and I have never admired a player as much as I admire Trevor Ford. In my opinion he is still the best centre forward in Great Britain. But he will never look like it whilst playing for the current Sunderland team as no one can tell me he is getting the support he deserves. The recent Davis for Ford switch at Portsmouth can

only be described as 'ridiculous'. The lion-hearted Welshman is surely the most determined player in a red and white shirt.

Ronnie Burns
Heddon

What is wrong with Sunderland? Against Aston Villa Snell did the work of three men in midfield, yet Shackleton strolled around as though we were 5-0 up. Then what do we see against Portsmouth? Snell dropped and Shackleton allowed to go on. There is no doubt about Shackleton as an entertainer is the best in the country but as a worker in a team he is a non-event. Trevor Ford with the right support is the best centre forward in Britain. Does he not prove it in every game he plays for his country? Why has his play declined since he came to Sunderland? I for one would hate to see Trevor Ford leave Sunderland. So come on those other forwards, think less about personal gain and give Trevor the service he needs

M. J. Shotten
Sunderland

With the press and fans desperate for more info on the impending transfer, Trevor was back in the team against Blackpool and the 60,000 fans who gave him fantastic applause as he took to the pitch at Roker Park. With Shackleton out injured, the Black Cats won 3-2 as Trevor repaid the fans with two goals. Trevor continued in the side, on and off mainly due to an ankle injury. The injury was a relief for manager Murray as he also had Shackleton nursing an injury, which meant he could hopefully keep them apart for a while. Nothing, it appeared, was happening regarding the transfer; the club did not seem to want to let him go. While out injured, Trevor noticed Cardiff City manager Cyril Spiers in the directors' box for the home game against Middlesbrough. Trevor knew what may be happening and his thoughts drifted to a life back in south Wales. After the game he was invited into the boardroom where chairman Ditchburn told him that Cardiff City were keen to sign him. Ditchburn then told him that he would come to Trevor's house along with Mr Murray and Mr Spiers. Trevor leapt into his car and drove home to tell Louise the news. He knew that she would follow him anywhere and this was in some way reward for all her support over the years. The doorbell announced the arrival of Ditchburn and his colleagues. Louise made tea and the forms were put in front of Trevor. He looked at them and said that he had made some very good friends in the area, but he knew it was the right thing to do. Picking up the pen he signed and became a Cardiff City player. After signing he asked the room 'how much?' And they replied in unison, £30,000. Aperantly Cardiff had put in a bid days before, but the bid was rejected by Sunderland. However, the club did say that it might be worth Cyril Spiers travelling up to Sunderland to discuss the matter. Spiers did just that and Sunderland told him they would not to take less than £30,000 for the Welshman. Spiers then put through an urgent call to Cardiff City where club officials told him to 'pay whatever Sunderland want. We want Ford.' The news spread like wildfire among the press and the football community. The whole deal had been shrouded in secrecy and Trevor was happy to be coming home to Wales. He went back to the Sunderland training ground and said goodbye. Even Shackleton wished him well. He then phoned a friend at the *Sunderland Echo* and told them he wanted something put in the paper to thank the fans. That evening Trevor's thoughts appeared in print:

I should like to say thank you through the medium of your columns. A big thank you to the many Sunderland supporters who have given me encouragement during my period with the club. I should like them to know with all sincerity I gave them my thanks for their support and say that it is with real regret that I leave the Sunderland club, but as my style of play does not fit in its better that I go.

The best of luck to Sunderland Football Club and may they have a rapid climb up the ladder. They have the players, they have the supporters, and I am sure this can be done.

To all personal friends in Sunderland and the district, best of luck for the future.

Yours sincerely,
Trevor Ford

And so Trevor and his young family packed their bags for Cardiff.

Looking back at his time at Sunderland, many will ask why they bought him? Well, the only answer is that they just could; at the time they could buy whoever they wanted. Unfortunately this did not guarantee the club any success. When you look at the side during that time it was full of internationals and it is unbelievable that the side did not win an FA Cup or bring home that elusive First Division title. Many will look to the relationship between Trevor and Shackleton: although the two getting on would not have guaranteed silverware, it certainly would have made it more of a possibility. The two plainly never saw eye to eye and there were obvious mistakes made by both parties in their squabble. Many feel there was an element of jealousy by Shackleton towards Ford. He was popular within the dressing room, the directors liked him, he looked like a film star and he had friends in the press. And subsequently maybe Ford was jealous of his Shackleton's talent and godlike status with the fans. They were very different players who would have complemented each other well. It's testimony to Trevor that he made 117 appearances for the club and scored seventy goals in his time at Roker Park. Imagine how many he would have achieved if the pair had worked together? The only real losers in the whole affair were the Sunderland supporters who really deserved more from both players. Bill Shankley, former Liverpool manager, once said that football teams are like a piano: you need ten to carry it and one to play it. It was obvious that Sunderland had two players who wanted to play, and that was never going to work.

8

Back Home

When Trevor arrived at Ninian Park in December 1953, Cardiff City had just won 3-1 at home to Liverpool. The win was a welcome relief for manager Cyril Spiers and his men as the Bluebirds had just come off the back of three horrendous results, losing 4-0 away at Newcastle United, 6-1 at home to Manchester United and 6-1 away at West Bromwich Albion. But the Ford signing had certainly appeased the supporters who were looking for the club to stop the rot. The club had been promoted to the top division in the 1951/52 season after an absence of twenty-three years, and the fans were keen to push on for the title. Manager Cyril Spiers had collected together a decent side with Alf Sheerwood as captain as well as players Ken Chisholm, Charlie Rutter, George Edwards and Stan Montgomery, along with a smattering of youth such as Alan Harrington, Colin Baker, Graham Vearncombe and Cliff Nugent.

The signing of Trevor Ford by Cardiff City took the whole of the football world by surprise. Many clubs later expressed an interest in the Welsh international, but it was the Bluebirds who acted swiftly and got the deal sorted, although Trevor was not the club's first choice by any means – they had tried to sign the young John Charles from Leeds United and after that failed they went after Barnsley's Tommy Taylor, again to no avail. The move was a no-brainer as far as Trevor was concerned: Cardiff were in the top division and it was a chance to come home and live in south Wales. This was also music to Louise's ears as she was expecting the couple's second child and would be happier with her family around her. Trevor signed for £15 per week and £12 in the summer; he was also sorted out with a job as a rep with Harris Paintbrushes, who were based in Cardiff. The move also allowed him to get involved with Glamorgan cricket club during the summer months.

Trevor had become Cardiff City's big signing and was one of the most recognized sportsmen of the day. He and Louise were invited to various functions, not just in Wales but all over the UK. While at Cardiff, Trevor struck up a friendship with comedian and actor Stan Stennett and his wife Elizabeth. Stan, being a Cardiff lad, was also a regular at Cardiff City games, particularly in the directors' box. They hit it off immediately, as did their wives. Stan was a larger-than-life character who loved interacting with people. He had a bit of mischief in his eye and many a time he would come down to the dressing room to entertain the players. Wales and Cardiff midfielder Colin Baker remembers it well: 'Trevor and Stan were inseparable. They were really good mates. Stan came into the dressing room once with a bow and arrow through his head and told us that the fans were not happy so we should go careful. We all fell about laughing.'

Everything appeared to be perfect, but this period in Trevor's career would turn out to be pivotal. There were early rumblings when the signing was announced. It's alleged that chairman Sir Herbert Merrett did not want to sign the cheque for Ford, as he had been told that the striker was trouble. Despite this, Merrett did sign, as for all the gossip he was a businessman who knew Ford would put bums on seats at Ninian Park and catch the imagination of the Cardiff supporters. Certain players had also expressed uncertainty about the arrival of Ford, feeling that he was a 'big-head' who would upset the training-room harmony – it was obvious the tales from the Sunderland dressing room had spread like wildfire among the players. Cardiff City and Wales international Alan Harrington remembers Trevor with affection:

I remember meeting him in the hotel in Sheffield before his debut at Sheffield Wednesday. I knew Trevor from his exploits with Wales and I was really excited to be playing with him. I was only a young kid, yet he was really friendly with all the lads, although a couple of the older players were whispering that he was a 'big-time Charlie'. But really that couldn't've been further than the truth. He looked and carried himself like a star. Myself and the

other young lads really looked up to him. He always had time
for people and I think underneath the expensive clothes he was
just a lad from Swansea who was a bit shy.

There was to be no repeat of the striker's famous home debut
against Sheffield Wednesday when playing for Sunderland. Again
there was mass media interest in the Welsh international's debut,
but the Bluebirds went down 2-1 with Ken Chisolm getting the
Cardiff goal. As usual, Trevor was frustrated that he did not score.
The local press were more forgiving, writing:

> Ford showed rare soccer skill and a refreshing determination to
> shoot at every opportunity. Unfortunately the service he received
> was poor and by next week the City will have to devise ways and
> means of bringing him into the game more.

The following week Cardiff entertained Middlesbrough at Ninian
Park. Merrett and the rest of the Cardiff board were well aware
of the pulling power of their new acquisition. A gate of 30,000
crammed into the ground – 10,000 more than the previous home
game against Liverpool – as fans flocked to see the Welshman's
home debut. As the teams ran out, an almighty roar greeted Trevor
accompanied by an impromptu chorus of 'We'll keep a Welcome in
the Hillside'. Trevor's eyes misted up as he puffed out his chest and
promised himself he would pay back the crowd for their wonderful
reception. Pay them back he did, getting on the end of a cross from
winger Mike Tiddy to win the game 1-0 for the Bluebirds. Alan
Harrington remembers the game:

> Trevor won over any doubters in the dressing room with those
> first two appearances for the club. Yes he was the star man, but
> he had the talent to deliver; he never stopped running and any
> players that were suspicious of him certainly never felt that way
> after playing with him. He always gave 100 per cent. He got stick
> when some of the board members came down to the dressing
> room and invited him up to the boardroom after the game for
> drinks, but he just laughed it off saying, 'I'm off to the Royal
> Box with people who know nothing of football.' Things like that
> showed he could mix with all sorts of people; he was never fazed

by whether you had money or not. I think that's why one of the board members fixed him up with a job repping for Harris. He was a real people person who would talk to anybody.

Weeks after Trevor's arrival at Ninian Park, strike partner Ken Chisholm put in a transfer request after being dropped from the side. Chisholm, who was a fiery no-nonsense Scot, felt that his goalscoring record did not warrant him losing his place in the side, and with this in mind he met with manager Spiers. The result of the meeting was that Chisholm was sold to Sunderland for £15,000. It appeared handy that Cardiff knew Sunderland were looking for a centre forward at the time. Chisholm told Trevor that he was genuinely upset to go as he felt they could have built up a great partnership together. Both players wished each other well. The transfer of Chisholm certainly played on the striker's mind as it looked as though he had left because of Trevor, but that could not have been further from the truth. There were even rumours that the Chisholm transfer was part of Trevor's transfer deal with Sunderland. Both clubs denied this, but it was certainly a distraction Trevor could do without. The club went through a mid-season slump, including a disastrous return to Roker Park for Trevor as Sunderland thrashed the Welshmen 5-0, one of the goals coming from Len Shackleton who milked the applause (perhaps as Trevor would have if the tables were turned). Trevor received a hero's welcome, but picked up a nasty knock on his ankle that would keep him out of the side for a few games. Sunderland's Stan Anderson remembers his return:

He was the usual old Trevor. He came to see some of the lads before the game and went around all the people who worked behind the scenes at the club to say hello. Cardiff were terrible that day, but he put himself about a bit as usual yet got no service. I was told he was up in the boardroom after the game with the Sunderland directors hanging on his every word. They still loved him at the club, but I'm not sure how the Cardiff directors felt, particularly after losing 5-0, their star man entertaining the opposition. Players like me never got invites to the boardroom; that was reserved for players like Shack, and I think he declined when he knew Fordy was going up there.

Cardiff recovered early in the year with a hard-fought 1-1 draw with Arsenal at Highbury with Trevor scoring his second league goal for the Bluebirds. After the game, manager Spiers told him he wanted to see him for a chat after training on the Monday. Trevor went into the meeting with certain trepidation, as he knew he was struggling in front of goal since his signing. Spiers told him 'You're not getting the sort of passes that you need, Trevor; the sort from which goals are scored. So we have devised a scheme under which you will do the foraging and lay on the pass for others to score.' Surprisingly, Trevor agreed, as it was best for the team; he knew it would mean he would have to alter his game totally. He would get a free role, which was good, but he would be covering a lot more ground at the expense of his goal tally. He also was worried what effect the change could have on his role as Wales' number nine. Trevor agreed to give it a go at least until the end of the season.

With the change, Cardiff proceeded to win seven of the next eight games, including victories away at Manchester United, Tottenham Hotspur and Liverpool, and a win that relegated the Anfield club to the Second Division. Cardiff eventually finished in a respectable tenth place, although there had been disappointing exits in the FA Cup to Port Vale and in the Welsh Cup losing a semi-final 2-1 to non-league Flint Town. Trevor ended the season with nine goals in all, behind Ken Chisholm, who had bagged twelve before his transfer, Wilf Grant, who also had twelve to his name. It was an interesting return for the Welshman; he had changed his game for the good of the side but still kept his beloved number nine jersey. The club seemed happy as gates were averaging 30,000, and off the field Trevor was now the proud parent to two young lads as Louise had given birth to their other son, Martyn.

Trevor kept himself busy through the summer, repping and constantly listening to customers telling him where the club could improve. Trevor enjoyed the banter and he quickly realized that maybe this could be a real career when he hung up his boots. He was also approached by Glamorgan cricket to see if he would turn out for their second eleven as a bowler in friendlies or one-day games. He agreed and loved every minute, especially the 'expenses' they put his way. He found it quite comical that cricketers were open about what they earned as none of it was under the counter, which was a real contrast to football. It was well known that, for instance, cricketer Cyril Washbrook of Lancashire had a benefit match in 1948 that earned him £14,000 tax-free, yet footballers, whatever standard they played at, would get a payment of £750 when they retired (if they were lucky), which would be taxed. The inequality of the two sports made Trevor angry.

As the new season started there were massive changes throughout Cardiff City. Manager Cyril Spiers resigned, giving no real explanation of why, but later joined Crystal Palace. Replacement Trevor Morris became Cardiff City manager in May 1954. Morris had originally been signed by Cyril Spiers, but in a wartime match the Caerphilly-born player broke his leg and was forced into retirement. He became secretary of the club and was a surprise appointment, as he had no managerial experience. Morris was a quiet-spoken man but inside he had a tough resolve, which would be something the striker would test to the limit during his stay at the club. Morris met with Trevor and told him he wanted him to revert to his old ways as a bustling centre forward. Again the striker agreed whatever was good for the team. He was more than happy to go back to his bustling style as it appeared to bring him more goals.

There were no new signings pre-season, but the club did introduce local youngsters Don Clarke, Neil O'Halloran and John Davis into the squad. The new season started disastrously for Morris as the club lost 1-0 to Burnley at Turf Moor. Things did not improve for the next match at Ninian Park where they lost 5-2 to Preston North End, with Trevor opening his account along with Mike Tiddy. The Bluebirds redeemed themselves with their next game, winning 2-1 against Leicester City. Again Trevor found himself on the scoresheet, but this was at the expense of his ankle, which took a knock and which ruled him out of the next two games. Shockwaves went through Ninian Park as the club then lost 7-1 to Preston North End at Deepdale. Morris dipped into the transfer market, spending £12,000 on inside forward Ron Stockin from Wolverhampton Wanderers. Three draws followed before the club produced two wins on the bounce, winning 3-1 at Brammell Lane against Sheffield United and 3-0 back home at Ninian Park against Manchester City. Morris chopped and changed his side, bringing in youngster Islwyn Jones for the game against Sheffield United and winger Cecil Dixon in a 1-1 draw at Everton, eager to see what his best team was. Although the club was struggling, it appeared as the new year arrived that Stockin had become a worthy acquisition, netting seven goals since his arrival. Trevor's move back to an old-style centre forward role had seen him net twelve goals by the end of the year including a double in a 2-0 win at Aston Villa where he alone received a standing ovation from the Villa fans for his performance. There was to be no cup run for the Bluebirds as they bowed out in the third round of the FA Cup, losing to Arsenal 1-0 at Highbury because of a Tommy Lawton goal. The club though were still in the Welsh Cup after winning 7-0 against Pembroke, a game in which Trevor scored four times against Newport County. The cup had become very important to Trevor as he had still not won any trophy in his career and he figured at the moment this was his best chance of some silverware. The competition meant a lot to all the Welsh sides, which is why they played their strongest sides all the way through no matter who the opposition was. The chance to be Wales' top team and parade a trophy was also important to the fans, which is why attendances were averaging around the 10,000 mark for the early rounds. Trevor Morris went back into the transfer market, signing Coventry City winger Gordon Nutt for £12,000 and a young twenty-one-year-old blonde-haired striker from Kidderminster Harriers called Gerry Hitchens for £1,500 on a part-time basis, as he was still working as a miner in the Nantgarw pit near Pontypridd. The club knew Hitchens was a bit special, but they also realized he was not ready for the first team yet, even though he had scored twenty goals in thirty-eight games for the non-league club. Morris saw Hitchens as definitely one for the future.

Despite this, The Bluebirds crashed down the table and suffered a disappointing exit from the Welsh Cup in a 2-0 semi-final loss to Chester City. As the season was coming to an end, Morris and Cardiff City found themselves in a relegation battle. The fixture list could not have been worse for the Bluebirds as they found themselves with a home game against Wolves, who were neck and neck with Chelsea for the title. Defeat for the Bluebirds would surely result in an end to their First Division status. Morris decided to throw Gerry Hitchens into the mix, partnering Trevor up front. It was a bold decision from Morris, but he had faith in both Trevor and Gerry to get the goals.

Over 30,000 fans crammed into Ninian Park for the game. A win for Wolves would mean they had won the title and defeat would mean Cardiff would be relegated, so the stakes could be no higher. Alan Harrington remembers the dressing room:

> We were all incredibly nervous before the game. I remember Trevor sitting next to Gerry talking about what was expected of him. Trevor told him that he would sort Billy Wright out and how they would help each other. Trevor told him not to worry as he would look after him. I just had a feeling that we could do it as we were all pumped up for the game and we could hear the crowd outside. I know there was no love lost between Wolves manager Stan Cullis and Trevor, which I think dated back to Trevor's Swansea days. Cullis made a point of shouting 'Watch Ford, he will kick you if he gets the chance' in the tunnel before we came out. Trevor just took it as a compliment.'

The match was an absolute thriller. Gerry Hitchens scored on his debut after three minutes, Wolves came back, and Trevor had a fantastic tussle with England captain Billy Wright who he had crossed swords with on many a Wales v. England game. As Wright said in later life, 'He was one of the finest centre forwards of my generation, mixing good ball control with physical strength. We had many great duels during our career but always ended up hugging each other at the end of the games in which we had tried to knock the hell out of each other.' Together Ford and Hitchens were incredible, helping each other along with the rest of the Cardiff side. The Bluebirds eventually won 3-2 with Trevor scoring the other two Cardiff goals. The defeat meant that Chelsea won the league and Wolves finished second. Cardiff had saved themselves and went to Huddersfield for their final game of the season. The Bluebirds lost 2-0 with Gerry Hitchens replacing Trevor midway through the second half.

The emergence of Hitchens would be significant in manager Trevor Morris's thinking for the next few seasons, as he plainly saw the youngster as a ready-made replacement for Ford. Cardiff finished the season in twentieth place, which was disappointing for all concerned. Although they lost eight games at home, they were still averaging 25,000 fans per home game, which showed that despite the scare of relegation, the crowd had not deserted them. As for Trevor, he had become top marksman at the club with nineteen goals, which added to his kudos as top dog at the club. But during the summer his position at the club would be tested as Trevor fought again for something he believed in.

During the summer months the Cardiff City board became active in the transfer market, bringing in three players form Sunderland – inside forwards Harry Kirtley, Howard Shepperd and winger Johnny McSeveney, worth a combined £9,000. The club also said goodbye to greats such as Billy Baker, Stan Montgomery and George Edwards, who all retired. The clubs were obviously making huge changes in an attempt to stop last season's flirtations with relegation. Trevor arrived one May afternoon to sign his contract for the season and was told by manager Morris that his contract would be a sliding scale. Trevor looked flabbergasted. The sliding scale meant that the club would pay him £15 as long as he was in the first team, but only £13 if relegated to the reserves or injured. Trevor told Morris in no uncertain terms, 'If the club warrant me worth £30,000 in the transfer market, should they not consider me worth top wages?' 'Now don't be difficult Trevor,' replied Morris. 'Everyone in the team is being treated the same,' he went on. 'That's not the point,' replied the striker. 'Either I'm worth £15 or I'm not. If I'm not then I would sooner turn the game in as I can earn £15 without using my feet.' Morris replied, 'The directors have agreed on a sliding scale, that's the position we treat all players the same here.' 'Very well I'm not signing,' replied Trevor, walking out of the manager's office.

The stand-off between the two parties continued and as Trevor's contract ran out in May his wages stopped from there in. But this did not stop the striker taking his wife and family to Italy for a summer break. Trevor also spoke to some of his friends in the press, creating more stories about how Trevor Ford could be on his way out of Cardiff City. On the family's return from the Continent Trevor got himself ready for pre-season training in July. He arrived at the club not really knowing if he had indeed played his last game for them. Morris called him into the manager's office and asked if he would be signing. Trevor replied, 'Yes I will sign but only if I'm on top money.' Morris replied, 'I will get back to you.' Three days later the striker was summoned to an evening board meeting at the club. The club offered Trevor his lost pay and a contract based on what he was used to without the sliding scale. Trevor duly accepted but Morris and the board did not forget the head to head. Maybe Morris had chanced his arm in trying to push Ford out the door, especially as he knew he had a replacement in Hitchens waiting in the wings? He knew Ford would react in this way as the sliding scale challenged what Trevor was all about; it questioned whether he was good enough and that struck a chord the striker, and maybe Morris knew it would unnerve him. He also knew that Trevor's reaction would add to the reputation that Ford was difficult to manage, making him seem the bad guy with the fans. Some of the fans did indeed react negatively to Ford as the new season approached, calling him greedy and selfish – this was certainly something the striker had not experienced from his own fans before. The new season was certainly going to be a very lively one for Trevor and Cardiff City.

1. A young footballing star: Trevor with the Swansea School's Shield.

2. Aston Villa squad of 1949. Trevor is in the middle row, second from left.

3. FA Cup, 1951. Sunderland beat Norwich City 3-1. Trevor (airborne, right) is in the thick of the action, as always.

4. As most people remember him – a real snappy dresser.

5. Trevor in action for Sunderland.

6. In the red and white of Sunderland, Trevor prepares to batter another 'keeper towards the goal.

7. Sunderland v. Wolves, 1952. A 1-1 draw in the snow at Roker. Trevor tussles with the Wolves' defence.

8. 1954. The game ended in a 3-1 defeat for Wales at Ninian Park. Here we see Trevor competing for the ball with Yugoslavian 'keeper Vladimir Bear.

9. Wales team v. Yugoslavia 1954/55. From left to right, back row: Ivor Allchurch, Roy Paul, Jack Kelsey, John Charles, Dave Bowen and Alf Sherwood. Front: Billy Reed, Trevor Ford, Walley Barnes, Derek Tapscott and Roy Clarke.

10. Trevor flicks the ball past England 'keeper Gil Merrick to score one of his two goals for Wales in their 5-2 defeat at Wembley Stadium in 1952.

11. Trevor and Louise relax at a friend's wedding.

12. Relaxing at home, still in a suit.

13. Ford scores the first of his two goals in a Cardiff City 3-1 win against non-league Peterborough in the FA Cup.

14. Trevor in the strip of his new club PSV Eindhoven.

15. In action for Newport County against Brentford, October, 1960.

16. Ford and teammate Les Riggs watching from the Newport County bench.

17. Trevor in action for PSV Eindhoven against Lokomotiva Zagreb.

18. Playing for Newport County.

19. Trevor and son David on holiday in Majorca, 1965.

20. Trevor and friend Stan Stennett before a charity football match.

21. Greats reunited at the Vetch, Swansea. Trevor and Ivor Allchurch hold up their favourite shirts.

22. The happy couple enjoying their retirement.

23. Trevor with Cliff Jones.

24. Trevor with Terry Venables and Lawrie McMenemy.

25. Two great strikers from different eras: Trevor with a young Alan Shearer.

26. A quartet that money could not buy. From left to right: Sir Stanley Matthews, John Charles, Jackie Charlton and Trevor Ford.

27. Two international legends: England's Nat Lofthouse and Wales' Trevor Ford.

9

Trouble in Store

With his contract sorted, Trevor continued to be a man in demand. Off the field he continued activities such as his work repping for Harris Paintbrushes and took advantage of various invites to functions, particularly with Stan Stennett at his side to entertain the fans who wanted to see one of Wales' most renowned footballers. While at one of these functions Trevor met writer Howard Green who had written for various newspapers over the years. He and Trevor went way back. In the past the striker had given stories in exchange for cash to some of the papers Green had worked for. Trevor always thought of the press as a useful tool, particularly useful when highlighting the way the game was structured against players. He also thought it was part of his job to let fans know what was going on at the club, and if he could earn a few quid in the process there was no harm done. Green approached Trevor with the idea of writing a book about Trevor's life to date. Trevor never dismissed the idea but he thought things over with Louise. There had been a few autobiographies of various players, but they were rather bland and you got the feeling that the player never had any input of his own when writing them. After a few meetings Trevor agreed, telling Green that he wanted to do it properly and tell the public what the game was really like, and also tell the football authorities how they could improve. Green told the striker that he would get back in touch later in the season so they could start work on it.

Back on the field Cardiff City opened their 1955/56 account against the striker's old club, Sunderland, at Ninian Park. With the ground packed with 36,000 fans, the Bluebirds put on a wonderful display to win 3-1. Ex-Sunderland player and summer signing John McSeveney scrored two of the goals and Trevor added his first of the season with remarkable bravery, putting his head where others wouldn't. The local press wrote of Ford's performance:

> He may well be the bad lad of Welsh Football but it's impossible to imagine Cardiff City with a braver player than Ford. As he did last season, he leads the attack with such bravery and power that surely Sunderland must ask why they let him go.

Unfortunately for Trevor, he gained another injury during the win. This was something he was getting used to, after all the way he played the game had not really changed since he was a raw eighteen-year-old kid at Swansea Town and now he was in his thirties his body was certainly taking the punishment. As for manager Morris, this was no real problem as he had a ready-made replacement in youngster Gerry Hitchens waiting in the wings. With Ford injured, City lost their first away game of the season 3-1 at Arsenal. Trevor returned for the trip to Villa Park but his ankle was not really ready as Cardiff gained a 0-0 draw and the striker ruled himself out for the next four games. This included a dreadful 9-1 defeat at home against Wolves. The defeat shattered the team and the fans as the club lost the next two games away at Manchester City and Bolton Wanderers. Manager Morris tinkered with the side and decided to bring back a fit Ford with Hitchens playing alongside him. Trevor enjoyed playing with the youthful Hitchens and he felt a sense of protection with him on and off the field of play. Many a time Gerry would ask Trevor for advice, not only on the field but also off it, particularly about looking after the money side of the game, telling the youngster, 'Make as much for you and your family as you can.' On the field Trevor used to say to him 'I will do the thinking, Gerry, and you do the running.' The partnership also sparked the imagination of the fans, particularly after the game against Wolverhampton Wanderers last season that saved the club from relegation. The fans were desperate to see them play together again. Alan Harrington remembers the two players together:

> I think Trevor felt like a sort of fatherly figure to Gerry. Although he wasn't really that much older than him, Fordy would always be telling him advice about different opponents; even when Trevor was injured he would always come down to the dressing room before kick-off and tell Gerry about the centre half he would be playing against. Trevor took real pride in being the number one striker at the club.

The move worked and Cardiff ended their barren run, beating Sheffield United 3-2 at Ninian Park with Trevor and Gerry netting a goal each along with a rare Alan Harrington strike. Trevor continued to lead the line but Morris chose Harry Kirtley and Roy Stockin to support him, leaving Gerry as replacement when Ford was injured. During the next few games, Trevor found his scoring boots getting four goals in four games before picking up an injury in a 1-0 defeat at home to Manchester United. Trevor returned two weeks later for the draw with Tottenham Hotspur at White Hart Lane before missing the next two games again.

Trevor was fit for the next game at home to Birmingham City and was very much looking forward to meeting up with his old adversary in goalkeeper Gil Merrick. Trevor reported for training on the Tuesday before Saturday's game and went straight through to the physio's room to have his ankle checked over. After getting the all-clear he was met by Trevor Morris, who told him that he might be needed to play inside-left on Saturday with Gerry Hitchens playing at Trevor's beloved number nine. Trevor stopped in his tracks and as Morris walked away the striker thought long and hard about the comment. Did he mean it? Was he just trying to gee me up for the game, after all he had been out injured and was not really pulling up any trees in front of goal this season, so maybe it was just man management and his way of getting me fired up. Trevor went home and thought no more about it. On his return to Ninian Park on the Thursday Trevor looked at the team sheet posted onto the wall. As the players crowded round in a huddle, Trevor walked towards the noticeboard. Seeing Trevor a few of them walked away muttering to themselves; as they parted he could see, in black and white, 'HOWELLS, STITFALL, SHEERWOOD, HARRINGTON, SULLIVAN, BAKER, WALSH, KIRTLEY, HITCHENS, FORD, DIXON'. Trevor was in fact playing number ten alongside Gerry Hitchens at number nine. Alan Harrington remembers the day:

> We were all shocked. No disrespect to Gerry who was a worthy number nine, but Trevor was always our number nine. Trevor had played inside right with John Charles for Wales but he would've played anywhere for Wales to be honest. I think this was a point of pride on his behalf and I think Morris was testing him to maybe show that he was not committed to the cause. I don't think Morris forgot the problems they had with his contract at the start of the season.

Trevor went to see Morris immediately and asked him if anything could be done about the team selection for Saturday? 'No,' replied Morris. Trevor responded by telling him, 'Well I am sorry about that, but as I was not an inside left I did not intend to play at inside left.' 'How do you know?' he countered. 'You have never played there.' Trevor then told him 'I have been in the game long enough as a centre forward to know that I would not be suited anywhere else. I have not been transferred to Cardiff City to be messed about from one position to another and if the board and yourself do not consider my form good enough for a first-team appearance at centre forward, then I was quite prepared to play centre forward in the reserves.' The exchange became more and more heated as Morris snapped, 'You are paid by the club to do as you are told.' Ford replied, 'I am not playing at inside left. And I am giving you plenty of warning so that you can have another player standing by to fill the spot.' Trevor then walked out. When Trevor got home he was fuming. He was incredibly angry that Morris had told him to 'do as you are told', and he kept asking 'who does he think he is?' He was not prepared to be treated like a little kid. He talked things out with Louise and calmed down. That evening he phoned Howard Green and made arrangements to work on the book. Green told him that he had secured a publisher and was negotiating to serialize the book in one of the national papers when it was released next year. He also told him that another journalist,

Harry Pashley, who like Green had worked on the *Empire News* and *Sunday Chronicle*, would help him during the process. As far as Trevor was concerned, it could not come fast enough. Saturday arrived and Trevor arrived at Ninian Park an hour before kick-off, as usual. My own father, Glyn, was in the Cardiff City colts' team at the time and remembers the tension of the day:

> As young fifteen - and sixteen - year - olds the colts were essentially the clubs schoolboy side and we idolized Trevor. He looked like a film star, and even though we were young kids he always had time for us and asked us about our progress at the club. We would attend match days and clean the changing rooms and any other jobs that needed doing. Rumours were rife about Fordy not agreeing to play, and there were real tensions behind the scenes. We were hanging around waiting for Fordy to confront Morris. Some of the players asked us to see what we could find out. We couldn't believe Trevor Morris would stand up to him like that. Again he was a quiet-spoken man who encouraged us kids whenever he could. He certainly showed some balls when taking on Trevor.

The two men eventually met in a corridor by the tunnel. 'It's time for you to start getting changed,' Morris told Trevor. 'What position am I playing in?' he replied. 'Inside left.' Trevor just shook his head. 'I am sorry then; I'm not playing.' Trevor then walked to the dressing room and told the lads. He then got into his car and left for home. When Louise saw him pull onto the drive she knew that he had made his mind up regarding the matter. Trevor then listened to the Cardiff game on the radio. Cardiff City won the game 2-1 with Harry Kirtley and Colin Dixon getting the goals. As he stood in the front room looking out of the window he knew that this incident had not ended for either him or the club. When the news came out, the papers were full of it, and although Trevor had put his side of the story to various journalists, there was much condemnation from players and fans for what the striker had done, suggesting it was typical of Trevor's relations with the press that he sold his story to one of the national papers for a month's salary so he did not lose out financially. There were also accusations that he was jealous of Cardiff's rising star Gerry Hitchens, one claim that really got to Trevor. As far as he was concerned he liked Gerry and wanted to help him in any way he could, yet on the face of it that's exactly what it looked like to the man in the street. People said he was finished at Cardiff and at Wales. There was also some truth in this as he was fighting internationally with John Charles for top spot and now his place at Cardiff City seemed under threat. Cardiff's Colin Baker remembers it was a difficult time for Trevor: 'I remember getting in contact with him after the Birmingham game just to let him know that we still had high regard for him. We never took what he did personally. I know the papers had a field day calling him all sorts.'

One person who did come out and condemn Trevor's actions was Professional Footballers Association chairman Jimmy Guthrie, a one-time supporter of Trevor. Guthrie went on the television and said, 'Trevor Ford will get no support from us for his actions.' On hearing this Trevor resigned from the union with immediate effect, telling them that they did not have all the facts regarding the matter. As for Cardiff City, they informed Trevor by letter that he would be suspended for two weeks, and luckily there was to be no fine and he was not placed on the transfer list, a decision very much taken on the fact that the board still wanted him around. Trevor accepted the club's decision and continued to train with the club, but relations were very frosty towards the striker, particularly with Morris and the board. In total the striker missed five games. The break from football allowed the Trevor to work with Green on the book and he enjoyed recalling tales and putting his views about how the game could be improved across. It also allowed him to get some things off his chest, particularly regarding the football authorities and, of course, Len Shackleton. Cardiff dipped into the transfer market during his absence, gaining the signature of tough Dundee United defender Danny Malloy for £17,000. The club had struggled to replace 'legend' Stan Montgomery since his departure the previous season and Morris figured that Malloy would add some much-needed steel to the defence, which he certainly did. In his excellent autobiography *Memoirs of a Hard Man*, Danny talked about his first impressions of Ford and the fallout from the Birmingham game:

Fordy found himself in real bother. There was talk of a hefty fine, even rumours that he was to be transfer listed. The feeling in the camp was split. A few players who did not think much of Trevor thought a lot less of him after the incident. I believe some of the players viewed him as a big-time Charlie. Also I had heard about a bit of previous between some of the older lads and Fordy when he was at Sunderland. It was fair to say that they were less than chuffed when he signed up at Ninian Park. Personally, I got on really well with Trevor and had a lot of time for him. And I would much rather have played with him than against him any day of the week.

During Trevor's absence from the team the Bluebirds only lost one game and Gerry Hitchens had coped admirably in the number nine role. Yet with only one goal to his name in those five matches, it was clear that he needed a target man to play off and that was obviously Trevor. Whatever your opinions about the Ford and Hitchens situation, it was clear that together they were a phenomenal partnership. Trevor returned to the side for the away trip to Chelsea. He was given the number nine shirt and Hitchens played at number eight. The game ended in a 2-1 defeat for Cardiff but Trevor had laid on a goal for Hitchens, so it seemed as though the pair had started where they left off. For the following game away at Wolverhampton Wanderers, Gerry swapped over to the number ten position at inside left with Trevor again at number nine. The game was an important one for the side as they wanted to avenge the dreadful 9-1 battering that Wolves had inflicted on them earlier in the season. Cardiff City played exceptional that day and played the Midlands club off the field with a 2-0 win, goals coming from both Trevor and Gerry. The win ended Wolves' unbeaten two-year home record. The constant booing of Trevor from the home supporters after a heavy tackle on Wolves and England star Billy Wright marred the game. For the striker it was water off a duck's back, as he said after the game when asked about the barracking: 'I must be doing something right if the opposition are booing me.'

The new year saw the partnership in fine scoring mode as City defeated Leeds United 2-1 in the FA Cup along with a 9-0 win at Pembroke Borough in the Welsh Cup, a game in which Trevor scored four and Gerry hit a hat-trick. Trevor was staying fit in the league, playing as much as he could and turning out for Gloucester City on one occasion in a friendly against Portsmouth. This was nothing strange as it was a common occurrence in those days for a player to 'guest' for a non-league side to help with fitness. Gloucester lost the game 2-1 in front of a 6,000 crowd and showed their appreciation of the Welshman in the programme notes: 'Sincere thanks to our guest forward, Welsh international and Cardiff City striker, Trevor Ford. Trevor, who has played for some of the greatest teams in England and Wales and is a world-class centre forward.'

Back at Cardiff, Gerry and Trevor were experiencing a long stint in the side. As their partnership grew so did the goals, and by April the pair had notched thirty-nine goals between them in all competitions since Trevor's ban. Gerry had scored twenty-four and Trevor fifteen, and although the clubs were still far from safe in the league, they were on the verge of some silverware as they found themselves in the final of the Welsh Cup against Swansea Town. Trevor was ecstatic as it was a chance to win his first trophy in the game. Cardiff City finished the season in seventeenth position with Manchester United winning the league. Gerry was top marksman with twenty-eight goals and Trevor was behind him with twenty-two.

Cardiff's final game of the season was the much-anticipated final of the Welsh Cup. Cardiff had not won the trophy since 1938 and for what many believed was Wales's top side, their performance in the competition had been poor over the years. The game certainly caught the imagination of the supporters as 37,000 crammed into Ninian Park on that April evening – an attendance that is still a record to this day. Trevor had been named captain after Alf Sherwood had departed for Newport County. Welsh international Sherwood was considered a 'legend' at the club after joining in 1941. He rarely put a foot wrong for both club and country and gained thirty-nine caps in the process. Trevor was overjoyed to be asked by Morris and he loved the responsibility and hoped he could carry it into next season. City legend Colin Baker remembers the game:

I was only young at the time and I had just really broken into the side. The Welsh Cup final was certainly the biggest game I had played for Cardiff City up until that time. I remember looking around the dressing room and Trevor gave us a rousing speech about how he had won nothing in the game even though he had played at the top and for some very good sides, and he was going to make sure we were going to take the cup home. There wasn't really the fierce rivalry that Swansea and Cardiff have today. Lots of the lads knew each other and some were Wales teammates, but we were all fired up for the game.

City lined up with Vearnacombe, Stitfall, Sullivan, Harrington, Malloy, Baker, Walsh, Kirtley, Ford, Hitchens and McSeveney, and the Swansea Town side boasted names such as Ivor Allchurch, Mel Charles, Des Palmer and Johnny King. Both teams started well, but the Bluebirds struck the first blow in the thirteenth minute when Brian Walsh cut inside the Swansea defence and curled a shot right into the top corner of Johnny King's goal. With Cardiff on top, things suddenly turned in Swansea's favour. Cardiff's Harry Kirtley went into a challenge with Swansea's Thomas, the result of which was that Kirtley broke his leg. Baker recalls, 'We could see Harry was in pain as he limped off but we had no idea the leg was broken. We knew we would be up against it as we were now down to ten men as there were no substitutes then.' Despite the setback, Cardiff went 2-0 up when McSeveney headed home a Walsh cross. Cardiff went 3-0 up early in the second half after great work by Ford set Walsh in to secure his second goal of the game. Cardiff were cruising until seventy-eight minutes in, when Kiley got one back for the Swans. The goal seemed to give hope to Swansea and the confidence just seemed to drain from Cardiff as Des Palmer scored a second, the game now at 3-2. Luckily for the Bluebirds the referee blew the whistle. Cardiff had won and Trevor achieved his first trophy. The forward led the team up the steps of the grandstand at Ninian Park to collect the cup. As he lifted it the whole ground cheered and clapped; even the Swansea fans applauded a great game.

After the presentation the team drank champagne in the dressing room. Trevor embraced manager Trevor Morris and for a few moments the two of them laughed and joked together. All the problems they had encountered during Trevor's time at the club seemed to be forgotten in an instance. Trevor, along with some of the other lads, went into the centre of Cardiff to celebrate, but they made time to stop at the hospital to give Harry Kirtley his winner's medal. The players ended up in a restaurant in the city centre and were later joined by their wives and girlfriends. Alan Harrington, another member of the side, remembers the night:

> We had a great time enjoying our success. I remember Trevor making a speech in the restaurant where he told us all how proud he was to be the captain and how he hoped we would win more silverware. Typical of Trevor though, he left midway through the night with some of the directors while we all just had a party.

The summer would turn out to be a busy one for Trevor. He threw himself into the book with author Howard Green, a book they decided would be aptly called *I Lead the Attack*. Trevor knew some of the content would be red-hot for the establishment, but he felt so strongly about how footballers were treated that he thought the only way he could force the change for the next generation would be to lift the lid on what was really going on. Sportsmen were just starting to bring out books at the time and Trevor wanted his to be like no other. He and Green met the publishers, Stanly Paul in London, and it was agreed that the book would come out the following year, in 1957. In addition, a few months before its release, it would be serialized in one of the national papers, earning Trevor a cool £6,000 – a colossal amount at the time. He would also get a royalty based on sales of the book. Trevor realized that his career, although still at the top in terms of club and country, would be a short one like for so many footballers, and he had been around the game long enough to see so many footballers end up with nothing after their clubs had finished with them. He vowed early in his career that it would not happen to him. He knew the book would be controversial, but he looked at it as a last big payday. Little did he realize that the events of the following season would, to some, determine his legacy forever.

10

The Fallout

Trevor and his young family spent the end of the summer on the beaches of the Italian Riviera. Foreign holidays were very important to him as he looked upon it as an education, particularly for his young sons. Trevor loved experiencing different cultures and he enjoyed the Continental lifestyle, and of course the clothes. He would spend hours talking to Louise about what their life would have been like if the transfer to Fiorentina had gone ahead a few years ago. When he returned to the UK he had more meetings with his publisher about the content of the book. The main worry for publishers Stanly Paul was the acknowledgement that players were the recipients of under-the-counter payments. Trevor was adamant that this had to go in the book. He explained that he had mentioned no names, but talked about the practice being open throughout football. He knew questions would be asked by the authorities, but his view was one of 'I have told you it's going on, now it's your job to find out by whom.' Trevor also wanted to highlight the way he was treated when he signed for Sunderland and ended up with a £100 fine off the FA. It was something that he had never forgotten. Howard Green was also concerned how certain aspects of the book would affect Trevor's present club Cardiff City. How would the players react to the facts about payments and criticisms of certain players Trevor had played with over the years coming out in a book, and would Cardiff City be furious that one of their players was, in the authorities' eyes, causing trouble. Trevor's response was one of 100 per cent belief that this was the right thing to do at this stage of his career. He informed the club that he had a book coming out and that it would be serialized in a national paper. The club were not too bothered; they evidently had no idea of the content of the book.

Trevor had been installed as captain for the new season and he was thrilled by the acknowledgement of the club, thriving on the responsibility it gave him. His only worry was whether it would affect his own performance up front. Trevor Morris relied on the same squad as last season for the opening encounter against Arsenal at Highbury. The Bluebirds earnt a hard-fought 0-0 draw and Trevor was pleased with him and Gerry Hitchens' display up front, although a goal from either of them would have made a perfect start to the season. City produced a breathtaking performance for their first home game of the season against Newcastle United. The Bluebirds won 5-2 in front of 42,000 with a goal from McSeveney, two from Nugent and a further two from Trevor. The dressing room was buzzing afterwards as the players congratulated themselves on a job well done. Many thought that this could be a very good season for the club. Another high-scoring game followed as Burnley were held 3-3 at Ninian Park. Again Trevor got on the scoresheet, along with McSeveney and Hitchens. Two further away defeats followed – 1-0 against Newcastle United and a 6-0 drubbing at the hands of Preston North End.

Trevor, by his own standards, was poor in both games, and although still in the number nine role, the pressure on him to deliver was gaining momentum. Many fans thought Trevor was finished and many called for Alf Sherwood to come back to the club as captain. A further two home games went by in which he failed to score – a 2-1 win against Sheffield Wednesday and a 1-1 draw with Chelsea. His form was concerning him; he had suffered longer spells without a goal but he was always in the game and at the moment he felt a bit of a passenger. Before the next game, against Sheffield Wednesday, Trevor went and spoke to Trevor Morris about the situation. In a complete turnaround from the previous season, Trevor said that he would give the number nine shirt to somebody else for the benefit of the team. Morris was certainly shocked, considering what had gone on before when selection was discussed. But Morris told him that he could see the striker was struggling but he wanted him to keep the jersey; he thanked him for acting like a captain. Cardiff lost 5-3 at Hillsborough with McSeveney getting two goals and Walsh adding a third. Defeat at Bolton Wanderers followed. There was a groundswell of fans who wanted the front line moved about and Gerry Hitchens was the popular choice for the number nine spot, especially as the youngster had been picked for the England Under-23 squad, which in itself was a real achievement. Again Trevor met with Morris and told him, as he had before, that he was willing to play somewhere else or even as centre forward in the reserves if the club could not accommodate him in the side. Morris again complimented him on his role as captain and thanked him for putting the team first, something that maybe the Trevor of old may not have done so willingly. Morris told Trevor he would think about it. On Thursday the team sheet was released for the forthcoming game away at Birmingham City and Trevor was moved from centre forward to inside forward with Gerry Hitchens taking Trevor's place. Cardiff's Alan Harrington remembers the dressing room before the game:

> Trevor was terrific. I remember when the team sheet went up we all looked at Trevor and expected him to cause a fuss. But we never knew he had previously spoken to Morris. To be fair he loved being captain of the club and I remember before the game he was clapping his hands and geeing us up as well as giving Gerry and young Neil O'Halloran, who was drafted in to the number ten role, advice.

It was clear that Trevor was not really happy being number eight; after all he had a book coming out soon entitled *I Lead the Attack*. And that's how he saw himself – taking punishment and not being a bit-part player. But there was a maturity to Trevor now. He was still getting niggles from his ankle that would mean he was not as quick as he once was. He could also see that just maybe he had a few years left in the game, and he was keen to enjoy them no matter where he played. Cardiff gave their all in the match at St Andrews and went in at half-time 1-1 with a goal from O'Halloran. In the second half both O'Halloran and Trevor had goals disallowed. This annoyed Trevor, especially as his old adversary, Gil Merrick, was keeping the Birmingham City goal.

Then Birmingham made it 2-1 and Trevor was told to switch with Hitchens and take the number nine slot. City could not pull the game back and lost 2-1. For Trevor, the local paper gave him a crumb of comfort, saying, 'When Ford went into the forward role the club suddenly had purpose in their play.'

Trevor returned to the centre forward role for the 0-0 draw at home with WBA as Gerry Hitchens made way. A wonderful display followed with a 4-1 win against Leeds United at Ninian Park. Gerry and Trevor were magnificent that day with Hitchens bagging two and Trevor and McSeveney getting the others. Things looked like they had finally clicked for the club, only for hopes to be dashed when they lost 5-0 to a young Tottenham Hotspurs team at White Hart Lane. It was a bad day all round, especially for Trevor, who aggravated his ankle and was forced to miss the following game away against Wolverhampton Wanderers. Trevor returned for the next game at home against Manchester City and they drew 1-1.

It was to be the very last time Trevor Ford pulled on a Cardiff City shirt, as the following Sunday *I Lead the Attack* was serialized in the *Sunday Express* and a bomb went off in the football world. As the papers arrived, Trevor's home phone never stopped ringing. Other journalists wanted to speak to him to try and get more out of the story, offering more money than rival papers for another exclusive. Trevor told them he had already signed a contract with the *Daily Express*. Howard Green also phoned to say things had gone crazy. The main bulk of the serialization was that players were getting money illegally from clubs and Trevor had told that he was 'looked after' at Sunderland, being offered jobs when he signed for them. He pointed out that this was not only at Sunderland but at most of the clubs. He also pointed out that when he signed for them, Chelsea had also offered money and perks, and when he turned them down they allegedly reported him and he was fined.

Despite everything, Trevor knew he had done the right thing. He received a call from Trevor Morris telling him the club wanted to see him in the morning, and knowing the Cardiff board like he did, Trevor had an inclination that they were not going to be happy. Trevor arrived at Ninian Park on the Monday morning as asked. He was met by Morris and went through the doors of the club and up the stairs to the boardroom, where some of the directors were waiting. After the pleasantries of asking if he was okay and whether he wanted tea, they got to the point and told him that, in light of the newspaper stories surrounding his book, they would be suspending him until further notice. Trevor explained that this had nothing to do with his performance on the field. However, it was also pointed out to him that his performances of late had been poor. The club told him he could train but would not be selected for the first team. He was also to go nowhere near the first team. Trevor was furious but maturity had taught him that a slanging match would be pointless. Morris escorted him down the stairs to his car. The manager told him how sorry he was and that it was the board's decision and not his. The pair shook hands and he left for home.

When he arrived home, Louise could see on his face that it was not good news. She made him a cup of tea and they talked about the decision. Trevor was worried it may harm his future with Wales, especially with a World Cup in Sweden in 1958 on the horizon. He convinced himself it wouldn't as he had not said anything particularly bad about the Welsh FA in the book. But what really stung was the mention of his poor form. A couple of years ago, when he refused to sign his contract, the club had given in, but this time it looked like that was not going to happen, maybe because he was not the asset he once might have been.

Trevor was summoned before a Football Association committee led by chairman Alan Hardaker and Burnley chairman Bob Lord, who had a fearsome reputation in the way he treated managers and players. On his arrival at the meeting in London both men tore into Trevor, asking him to name names, but Trevor just sat there and told them that it was not his job to name the clubs and players, it was theirs. He was telling them it was going on; now it was down to them to find out the rest. The pair ended the meeting and told him the decision would be quick. He waited for news and it came swiftly. He was to be banned *sine die*, which effectively meant he could not play again. Trevor was furious and told the press that no charges had actually been made against him. 'This is Britain,' he exclaimed, 'not an Iron Curtain country.' Colin Baker remembers the mood in the club: 'We all knew what Trevor was like but we were shocked at his punishment. I read all the stories in the newspaper and we all knew it was going on. Trevor never actually named anybody, only himself. He was a great loss to us and football.'

Trevor immediately put in an appeal. He had to use his own solicitors as he was no longer in the PFA, having resigned because of the criticism he received from chairman Jimmy Guthrie about not playing against Birmingham City. The cost of the appeal could run to four figures, but he and Louise thought it was worth it as it was his livelihood that was at stake. Trevor was devastated at the news, not only never playing for Cardiff but also losing the chance to pull on that red shirt of Wales. He felt so frustrated that he could be treated like that, and many people close to him felt some of the bitterness towards the authorities in the game that stayed with him all his life. Friends and family all rallied round, particularly friend Stan Stennett and his wife, who invited the couple to various charity dos they were involved in. Stan also started to organize some low-key charity football matches with his contacts and Trevor enjoyed kicking a ball around with a few ex-players. But it wasn't the same. He started to miss the competitive cut and thrust of football. Trevor was truly heartbroken at where he found himself.

As the new year started the bombshell of the Trevor Ford story just got bigger as the book was released. *I Lead the Attack* was not like any other football autobiography. They were usually bland pieces of work that concentrated on how players got to where they did and gave advice to youngsters on how they could do the same. There were no chapters about what actually went on at football clubs. Trevor's book was 157 pages and fourteen chapters. The book opened with a dedication to Louise and their sons, David and Martyn. Obviously the talking points from the book were the illegal payments, but the book was so much more. Trevor told us about how the Welsh FA worked and how they could be improved by maybe having a Welsh team that could play in the league and therefore help future players. He also talked about how grounds should change and how they should provide better facilities for the paying public to watch a match. He stressed that people should be in the warm, be able to buy hot food or have a drink before and after the game, maybe even hire cushions to sit on. He also gave us his opinion on the introduction of floodlights that were coming to the game. Many fans and clubs were sceptical of claims that people would go to games at night, but Trevor saw it as the future. All of this seems normal nowadays, but back then it was revolutionary. Trevor also gave his opinion of various players including Len Shackleton, who he believed had too much power at the club and was never a 100 per cent, ninety-minute player, something that many supporters agreed with. He also tackled the transfer system and how it treated players like pieces of meat, with the only winners being the club directors. It also gave him chance to comment on the treatment of Neil Franklin and the other players who had sought money abroad, and how other sports such as cricket allowed players to earn money tax-free when they retired whereas footballers' lump sums were taxed. These were the reasons for doing the book in the first place, and although it caused a storm, it was greeted in certain quarters as a look to the future.

The furore surrounding it also resulted in two letters arriving at the *Daily Express* and *The People* newspaper offices. The letters were from a mysterious Mr Smith who backed up Trevor's claims and mentioned goings-on at Sunderland Football Club, citing financial irregularities and undeclared payments to players at the club. Whoever Mr Smith was, he certainly knew the ins and outs of this great football club and his revelations would bring the club to its knees. The fire that Trevor's book started was growing, and at the end of January chairman Jimmy Guthrie was voted out from his post at the PFA to be replaced by Fulham player Jimmy Hill. Hill had started his career as an amateur with Reading football club before turning professional with Brentford. He certainly knew what he wanted. When once asked by a journalist, 'Do you think the abolition of the retain and transfer system would be good for the game?' Hill replied, 'I am not interested in the good of the game, only the good of my members.' Hill was middle class and had never asked for illegal extras in his dealings with his club Fulham, but he was young and had knowledge of business and would become a real asset to the struggle of footballers' rights. Hill made immediate contact with Trevor and told him he would help in any way to get his ban overturned. Trevor thanked him and told him he had his own people dealing with the matter, but maybe they could help each other along the way. The Football Association investigated the claims against Sunderland and subsequently went after them with a vengeance. The football league committee asked to see the club's books.

Meanwhile Trevor's appeal against his ban was scheduled for 3 March in London. When it came around Trevor went off to

London with his lawyers and also a letter from the PFA declaring that he had not in fact been charged with any offence. After numerous hours Trevor's ban was thrown out and he received with an apology from the FA. He was now free to play football again, although a return to Cardiff City certainly seemed out of the question. The board had no interest in having back 'Troublesome Trevor', even though the club were in a relegation fight at the time, a fight they eventually lost as they returned to the Second Division. Months later Cardiff sold striker Gerry Hitchens to Aston Villa for £20,000. Hitchens would go on and have an illustrious career for England, where he gained seven caps, and also in Italy playing for Inter Milan, Torino, Atlanta and Cagliari. City manager Trevor Morris lost his job the following season and headed for Swansea Town; Bill Jones replaced him at Cardiff.

Ford was contacted by one of the board members who had connections with the Philips electronic group based in Eindhoven, Holland. He told Trevor that local side PSV Eindhoven were prepared to offer him a four-year contract and a job promoting Philips products. PSV, which stood for Philips Sport Vereniging, or Philips Sport Union, were founded in 1913 as a way for employees of the Philips Organization to play football. In 1955 they were the first Dutch team to enter the newly formed European Cup, although they were knocked out by Rapid Vienna. Trevor and Louise mulled over the offer. Although everybody in football knew Trevor Ford was available to play again, it appeared his reputation as 'difficult' preceded him as there were no other real offers from clubs on the table, so in March 1957 Trevor decided to fly out to Holland for the week and see what the club was offering.

Eindhoven is a beautiful city around an hour's drive from Amsterdam. Trevor was put up in a hotel where he met PSV manager Ljubicha Brocic, a former Yugoslavian international who had played for Yugoslav Belgrade. There was real anticipation at the arrival of somebody with Trevor Ford's stature in the game and nobody seemed interested in the events that led to his original ban from the game. The Dutch league had gone professional in 1954 and the league was really looking for some big stars to attract. Trevor, if they got him, would be the first to grace the Dutch league. Dutch writer and PSV historian Frans Claes explains:

Trevor was well known to the Dutch fans as many of them knew him from his games for Wales and many of them also followed British football. They could not really believe that the one time most expensive player in football was going to sign for a Dutch league club. When he did sign the supporters loved him. Although many thought he was maybe past his best as he was now thirty-five years old. But the moment they saw him play he showed he had lost none of the stuff that made him such a great player over the years.

Trevor was offered a four-year deal of almost £100 a week, plus bonuses. He was also given, rent-free, a four-bedroom house on the edge of a forest. Philips Electrical would employ Trevor and his duties would be to attend various trade shows and promote the company – a type of representative role. He also knew that there would not be so many games as back in Britain – around thirty maximum compared to the fifty-plus at home. This would be a welcome relief for him, particularly considering his style of play and his continuing problems with his ankle. During the week Trevor looked at houses and attended the PSV game against FC Amsterdam as a guest of the club. The day after the match, Trevor was invited to join the club in a trip to Valencia, Spain, but a problem with Trevor getting a visa at short notice stopped him from travelling. Trevor returned home to see his family to discuss what he had seen. Two days later he went back to Eindhoven with Louise and they attended another PSV game, this time against Fortuna. Impressed with what he had seen, and how he was treated, he signed on the dotted line after the game and telephoned home with the good news.

When the couple returned to Cardiff he and Louise had much to sort out, particularly where the children were concerned. Louise, who was a stickler for education, thought the upheaval for David, now seven years old, would be too much so he was enrolled at Llandaff Cathedral School in Cardiff as a boarder. The family said goodbye to the likes of Stan Stennett and his family and invited many of their friends to come over to Holland when they were settled. It was particularly difficult for both Trevor and Louise to say farewell to their respective Mothers, but both of them knew it was an opportunity that particularly Trevor had always wanted. Even at the height of his fame he had always fancied going abroad to play. He wanted to experience other cultures and living in a different country was always his dream. He also realized that he would have to change his game as Dutch referees would not be as lenient as the British ones when it came to his style of play. The couple packed up their things, put the house on the market and headed off to a new life in the Netherlands.

Back home the fallout of both Trevor's book and Mr Smith's letters had come to a conclusion. The Football Association met with Sunderland directors at the Royal Victoria station hotel in Sheffield and three weeks later they were all summoned back to the hotel for their findings. The inquiry found that illicit payments had been made to players totalling £5,427. The club had paid contractors inflated prices for straw and tarmac. These payments were then returned to the club as treasury notes and then handed out to the players as payments, which at the time was illegal. The FA threw the book at Sunderland. Chairman Ditchburn and director Martin were suspended from any involvement in football ever again. Vice chairman Stanley Riston and director Lawrence Evans were suspended *sine die*. The club were also fined £5,000 and ordered to pay costs. Five players were hailed before the committee but they refused to answer any questions, as it would incriminate them and anyone else. The players Ray Daniel, Billy Elliott, Willie Fraser, and Johnny Hannigan were suspended *sine die* also, but after an appeal the ban was lifted. However, they were all made to forfeit any cash benefits on their retirement. Manager Murray was fined £200 but the commission took into account that he was operating on instructions. After an association with the club for over thirty years as a player and manager, he handed in his resignation to the new chairman in 1957. The elusive Mr Smith's identity to this day is still not known. For the PFA the whole affair paved the way for the maximum wage to be scrapped, which it eventually was in 1961, as Fulham's Johnny Haynes became the first £100 player.

Back in Eindhoven, Trevor and Louise we happily settling into life abroad. Trevor was happy with everything at the club, especially as he was treated like royalty by the fans. He and Louise would be stopped in the street whenever they went out as people welcomed them to the country. Trevor did not shy away from the attention either, becoming the proud owner of a convertible American Cadillac car with a personalized plate of TF32 that made him look every inch the superstar. As for Louise, well she was more than a little uncomfortable with all the attention. She enjoyed meeting the other wives but was never really happy with all the attention thrown her way. Trevor loved the continental way and enjoyed training with a passion. The basis of it was built around ball work and not too much running up and down just working on fitness, which was so typically the British way. He knew that this part of his career, even though it was towards the end, would make him a much better player. Even the kit was better; it was lightweight and breathable and did not get heavier as it got wet, like the kit at home. The shorts were shorter and shin guards lightweight. This also went for the balls, which were also lighter, and the boots were like carpet slippers, so soft, and supplied by a German company called Adidas. The boots were originally worn by the victorious 1954 World Cup winners West Germany, who created one of the game's biggest shocks by beating finalists and red-hot favourites Hungary 3-2 in the final. The company had designed the lightweight boot with a revolutionary screw-in stud for different types of pitch and weather. This was something that the West Germans had used to their advantage as the rain poured down before the 1954 World Cup final. The West Germans changed their studs; the poor Hungarians were stuck with fixed, nailed-in studs. Eventually the boot would filter in to the British game, but for Trevor this was a revelation.

Trevor made his debut on 3 May 1957 in a friendly at home against Lokomotiva Zagreb in front of around 30,000 fans. As he ran out in the red and white stripes he had a little chuckle to himself as he thought about his last debut in a similar red and white shirt playing for Sunderland. The reception he got from both sets of fans when his name was read out over the tannoy was terrific. Trevor was up front with forward Coen Dillen, who would go on to have legendary status at the club. Coen became great friends with Ford and certainly helped him adjust to the game. The Dutch international had been at the club since 1949 and he was the top scorer in nearly every season. The side was captained by Toon Brusselers, another Dutch international. His father was director of the Philips factory and he had been at the club since 1951, originally joining as a striker but moving to a more effective role in midfield. Hoping to supply the crosses for Trevor was Piet Fransen, a hot prospect who had been followed by many Italian clubs eager for his signature. He had refused any chance to move to Italy in favour of his native Netherlands. Manager Brocic was a tough guy who only knew but a smattering of English but his instructions to Trevor were pretty simple: 'Just get goals.' In fact, most of the team knew a fair bit of English and that helped Trevor immensely with matters on and off the field. The game ended with an 8-1 win for PSV. Trevor hit four goals for the Eindhoven club and became a huge hit overnight. It was the perfect start for the Welshman. As the season was over Trevor continually played friendly games in preparation for the next season, which certainly helped ease him into the Dutch game. These friendlies were against some of the top European sides of the day like Leeds United, FC Köln and Eintracht Braunschweig. In total, Trevor notched up twelve goals in eight games. He was an instant hit and his goalscoring exploits filled some of the British national newspapers' columns.

As the new season drew closer, Trevor and his family went back to Swansea to meet up with family. Everybody was very excited to hear about their new life abroad. The family met up with the Stennetts in Cardiff and Trevor and Stan acted like they had never been apart, laughing, joking and generally entertaining all around. When Trevor returned to PSV he was told that manager Brocic had been replaced with former Oldham and Middleborough defender George Hardwick. Hardwick was to also take over the national side in the Netherlands as well as coaching PSV. Trevor was delighted to have somebody from back home in the dugout, but he was sad to see Brocic go as he had a lot of time for the Yugoslavian. The reason given for his removal was just that the club wanted to try things with a British manager and maybe they thought they could get the best out of Trevor with a British man at the helm. PSV started the season against Sportclub Enschede. The game was a thriller for the fans as PSV lost 5-4. For Trevor, the game was one to forget. Not only had he not scored but also he injured his ankle badly, which kept him out for nearly two months. He was despondent as he really wanted to show Hardwick that he was still the fiery, rampaging Trevor Ford of old. Instead, he would have to sit out the next few games. While injured Trevor got on with his day job with Philips. Even though he was hobbling around on crutches, he always had a smile for people and mixed really well with the workforce. But in reality he was, like many sports stars, eager to get back to fitness. Throughout his time off with the injury the club were exceptional, and players and staff called in to the house to see how he and Louise were getting on.

Trevor returned to the first team in November of 1957. The club was home to GVAV and a good 25,000 fans had turned out to see Trevor Ford's belated home league debut in Dutch football. The game was a hard-fought affair, with both clubs competing for the win. Trevor, with his beloved number nine on his shirt, caused the opposing defence all sorts of problems as he attacked the ball whenever he could. The game finished 1-0 to PSV, and although he came close to getting off the mark, Trevor was pleased with his performance in light of his lay-off through injury. Fans only had to wait for the next game for Trevor's first league goal in the red and white shirt. Again it was a thriller as PSV went down 6-3 away at Blauw-Wit. Trevor grabbed a trademark header from outside the box, which left the opposition 'keeper in no man's land. The goal was typical: Ford won the ball at the halfway line and passed it out to the wing for young Fransen to cross back in the box where the Welshman was waiting. Despite the defeat, Trevor was on cloud nine. For Hardwick and his team, the start of the year was one of consolidation with two draws and a win. The end of January threw up a big test as PSV entertained giants Ajax at home. It was a test that the Eindhoven club would not be up to losing – an embarrassing 5-0. The local papers were full of anger towards the side but none was directed in the way of its Welsh star striker, even referring to him as 'the only one who tried in the game'. After the defeat, Trevor found his scoring boots, netting eight goals in eight games for the club.

However, as Trevor was finding his feet, the world of football was dealt a dreadful blow. The Manchester United team crashed at Munich airport on the way home from a European Cup game against Red Star Belgrade. There were seven player fatalities: Roger Byrne, Geoff Bent, Eddie Coleman, Mark Jones, Tommy Taylor, David Pegg and Bill Whelan, together with the three club officials, eight journalists and two other passengers. The news spread across the world and two weeks after the crash another of the team, Duncan Edwards, who had become a shining light in British football, lost his fight for life in hospital. Trevor was shocked and devastated; he had the utmost respect for Manchester United as a club. He had enjoyed some great games against them over the years and had played against some of the dead when on international duty. He phoned his friends in the press back in Britain and asked them to keep him informed of events. George Hardwick, seeing that Trevor was obviously affected by the tragedy, went to the press and declared that Ford could certainly do a job for Wales in the forthcoming World Cup in Sweden later in the summer. Trevor was thrilled with Hardwick's confidence in him, but unfortunately Hardwick's view fell on deaf ears as far as the Welsh selectors were concerned. However, the British press listened and started to mention the Welshman's exploits abroad. Trevor's son David remembers it well:

I was in boarding school at the time and I would go and see Mum and Dad every holiday. Both my parents were very keen that I got a good education. With Dad playing over in the Netherlands, my house tutor used to save the papers and read about how well he was doing over there, saying stuff like 'your Dad scored again, David'. I was really proud of him and so were my mates. It was interesting that the national papers had not forgot him. I imagine this was really due to the fact that he was doing his stuff in front of goal and they could not ignore him.

Trevor continued to find the net in his first real season in Dutch football as PSV finished a disappointing tenth in the league. Trevor had scored fourteen league and cup goals in twenty-two games, a reasonable return for somebody playing his first season abroad and particularly one in his thirties. Trevor had altered his game and was clearly no longer the crash-bang-wallop-type of player he once was. Now he had experience and knew when to make those all-important runs into the box and he had become a bit less savage when it came to defenders. He knew how foreign players thought and, bearing in mind he had been playing against some of the best in the world in his short time at PSV, that could surely go in his favour with the Welsh selectors considering the team on the edge of their first World Cup. He knew the fans and the press had not forgotten him. Hopefully the selectors could see there was a place for the Welshman, even in a bit-part role. Trevor waited with baited breath for the squad to be revealed, as did the fans who had never forgotten their one-time star striker.

11

Wearing the Dragon

Over the years there have been many labels placed on Trevor Ford – 'Fiery Ford' and 'Terrible Trevor' – names that seem to have followed him throughout his career. And although to a certain extent there may be some truth in those nicknames, let's not forget another label for Trevor, that of 'proud Welshman'. It is true the 1940/50s were different eras for footballers. Back then the most important thing a player could achieve in the game was to represent his country and win the World Cup. True Trevor loved the chance to earn as much money in the game as he could. He also loved the fame and all it brought with it. But to him there was no feeling quite like pulling on that red shirt of Wales, and for him that feeling never left him from his first international to his last.

It was always young Trevor's dream to be picked for Wales Schoolboys but, as described earlier in this book, his selection was cruelly taken away from him aged thirteen when he broke an ankle weeks before his debut against Scotland Schoolboys. And of course when he was fit enough to play he was too old for selection. The whole affair had a profound effect on the young Ford; he promised himself that he would one day wear that coveted Welsh shirt. His dream came true on 4 May 1946. Trevor had certainly carved a name for himself in the Swansea Town side with his goal prowess and as a result he was called to Swansea manager Haydn Green's office. Not entirely sure of why he was called to the office, Trevor went with a certain amount of trepidation. Green welcomed him and announced that the youngster had been picked for Wales in the forthcoming victory international against Ireland at Ninian Park. Speaking in his book *I Lead the Attack*, Trevor recalls the event:

> I was completely taken by surprise. My mind began to whirl as it dawned on me that I was at that moment on the threshold of the greatest ambition of every footballer, and I barely heard Mr Green as he added, 'Your play this season, Trevor, has been of the highest class and you deserve the honour. My congratulations.' It was some time before I replied. Although I knew the goals I scored for Swansea in my first in senior football had not gone unnoticed, the thought of landing an international cap so quickly had never entered my head. Green then said 'I know you will not let us down.'

With Haydn Green's words still ringing in his head, Trevor went to Cardiff to meet up with the squad and head of selectors, Mr Watts-Jones. The Welsh FA selectors were pleased to welcome the new 'star', but Trevor was full of self-doubt, particularly when he looked at the players around him in the hotel, players like Swindon Town wing-half Billy Lucas and Birmingham City's tough left-back, Billy Hughes. Lot of these Welsh players had seen the Welsh side through the war years and now a new breed of player was coming through, players like Cardiff City defender Alf Sherwood, Burnley forward Billy Morris, Cardiff City forward Roy Clarke and of course, the jewel in the crown, Swansea Town's 'wonder boy', Trevor Ford. Clarke, Sherwood and Morris were all included in the squad and it certainly helped when Trevor found out they would be making their debuts alongside him.

Trevor's debut in the red shirt of Wales clearly showed the Club v. Country problems smaller nations like the Wales were facing. It appeared that football league sides had scant regard for any other nation other than England and this caused problems for Wales, Scotland and Ireland in getting players released. A clause stated that players selected for England *must* be released, but players picked for the other home nations *may* be released. This was evident in 1930 when Wales played Scotland at Ibrox Park. As the Welsh team were not given permission by football league clubs to release their players, the Welsh team fielded on that day three amateurs, and not one player from the Football League Divisions one or two. Again Trevor's debut threw up the problem as he explained in his book:

I was incredibly nervous before the game as I paced around the Hotel. Then Billy Shortt, the Plymouth Argyle goalkeeper, walked over to me and it soon me began to dawn on me that here was a player in an even worse state than me. For Billy had been selected as reserve and the first choice 'keeper Cyril Sidlow of Liverpool was missing. He had still not turned up by midday, although none of us knew it; he was at that moment on a ship bound for America with the rest of the Liverpool team. Thus poor old Billy was kept until the last moment not knowing whether or not he was going to get his first cap. The Liverpool directors had not bothered to contact the Welsh FA. Half an hour before kick-off Billy was summoned to get changed.

A capacity crowd greeted the red of Wales and the green of Ireland as they marched out on that May afternoon. The Wales team were Shortt, Sherwood, Hughes, Warner, Jones, Burgess, Powell, Morris, Ford, Lucas, Clarke.

Trevor recalled that it was one of the most significant turning points in his career:

For twenty minutes or so I charged around looking for my first international goal. I chased the ball and chased after players. Then it came to me. As I flopped and floundered over the Ninian Park turf I saw myself in true light. I was just as much part of this international battle as a piece of flotsam wafted on to the field by a gust of wind, and as the match progressed I came to realize that here was a game far bigger and far harder than anything I had experienced before. For the first time in my life I was in a "big" game with "big" players and although I was tall and strong I felt like a dwarf amongst giants.

Part of the reason for Trevor's disappointing game was the experienced Irish centre half Jackie Vernon who, as they say, kept young Trevor in his back pocket all game. Jackie was a tough guy from Belfast who had earnt a glowing reputation for his performances with his club Belfast Celtic.

In every challenge Vernon was always a second ahead of young Trevor as he won the ball every time, and every time the ball was played up to the young Welsh striker, Vernon would nick it off him. Wales lost the game 1-0 with Tranmere Rovers forward Paddy Sloan scoring the all-important goal. As the whistle went Trevor trudged off the field before Jackie Vernon ran up to him and said, 'Don't worry son, you will make the grade.' Trevor never forgot the exchange between the two, and as he walked towards the changing rooms his head lifted with Jackie's words. Expecting criticism from the selectors, Trevor was amazed when Mr Watts-Jones said 'We never judge players on one appearance only. You will play in the opening international next season.' The kind words certainly lifted his spirits as he returned to Swansea, and days later it was found that he had in fact broken a rib during the game – probably a result of a tussle with Jackie. So with a battered rib, and even worse battered pride, Trevor could hardly wait for the next international to show what he could do.

That international was the very first full international after the Second World War, in October 1946. The venue was the Racecourse Ground, Wrexham, where Wales faced Scotland. Both teams fielded strong sides with Wales boasting the most costly footballer, Bryn Jones, who had signed for Arsenal from Wolverhampton Wanders for £14,000 in 1938. He partnered young Trevor up front. To compensate this, Scotland recalled tough Newcastle centre half Frank Brennan to the side, mainly to cope with the young Ford. The game was a typically frantic affair in front of 30,000 screaming fans. Trevor and Frank Brennen battled all game and the youngster certainly gave as good as he got, gaining Brennen's respect as the game went on. The game was poised at 0-0 after the break. Trevor won the ball at a corner and the ball fell into the path of Jones who smashed the ball home to put Wales 1-0 up. Ten minutes later Glasgow Rangers winger Willie Waddell pulled one back for the Scots. Then, with under ten minutes left, the ball was played up to Trevor, who managed to shake off Brennen and run towards goal. A quick one-two with Bryn Jones followed, and as the ball came back to him the young striker let fly and the ball screamed into the top corner. Trevor had scored his first goal for Wales. He raised both arms and was submerged by his Welsh teammates. With the game almost over, Scotland conceded a corner and, under pressure from Trevor, Jimmy Stephen, the Scotland captain, to put the ball into his own net to give Wales a 3-1 win. As the whistle blew, Trevor shook the hand of Frank Brennen. They exchanged pleasantries, and little did Trevor know at that time that he and Frank would do battle on a regular basis while wearing the black and white of Newcastle United and the red and white of Sunderland.

The goal for his country only added to Trevor's growing army of fans in the press. There was mounting speculation that he would be leaving Swansea for a bigger club. Sure enough, Trevor signed for Villa and sealed his arrival on the big stage with a goal in Wales 2-1 defeat against Northern Ireland at Windsor Park in the late spring of 1947. Trevor was certainly a breath of fresh air as far as the Welsh selectors were concerned. He epitomized the youth in a dogged Welsh team that had struggled against the Home Nations in the past, and had become the golden boy of the Welsh team. Due to his style of play Trevor was always going to pick up injuries in his league career, affecting his selection for the Welsh team. Villa were keen for him to represent his country and always tried to accommodate any Welsh FA request. A decent run in the Welsh team saw him make a further five appearances with a return of two goals. In May 1949 Trevor was given the opportunity of pitting his wits against foreign countries as Wales embarked on a tour of Portugal, Switzerland and Belgium. The idea of the tour was to get the players some international experience and hopefully invite the countries to play Wales the following year, earning some valuable money for the Welsh FA. Trevor was excited at the prospect as he believed facing continental opponents could only help his domestic game. Speaking in later life, he recalled the tour:

The whole tour was a disaster. I remember all the officials from the Welsh FA getting all the best treatment, yet us players were treated like servants. The flight to Portugal was terrible; we seemed to be bobbing up and down all the time. I thought Roy Paul was going to throw up all the way. I remember seeing the famous Lisbon stadium where the game was to be played. The pitch made Wembley look like a ploughed field. We could not wait to get started.

The game against Portugal was played on a lovely warm balmy Sunday evening. The Wales team were Hughes (Blackburn Rovers), Sherwood (Cardiff City), Lambert (Liverpool), Paul (Swansea Town), Jones (Everton), Burgess (Tottenham Hotspur), Griffiths (Leicester City), Lucas (Swansea Town), Ford (Aston Villa), Lowrie (Newcastle United) and Edwards (Cardiff City).

There were 50,000 crammed into the stadium and the noise was incredible. Trevor recalled:

There were soldiers on horseback riding around the outside of the pitch. After five minutes I put in a shot which sent the ball over the bar, but instead of the ball being returned to the field, the 'keeper got a smaller ball from the back of the net and carried on with that. There was chaos, as Roy Paul and George Edwards demanded to the referee that we use the original ball, but he waved them away. We were playing well, using our tried and trusted tactic of ball out to the wings then cross it in for me to get on the end of. This worked and I had scored two goals as we went in 2-1 at half-time. The first half had been a real education as the Portuguese players had spat, bitten, pulled shirts and tripped us whenever they got the chance, but the referee was not interested in any of our protests. The second half we seemed to lose all our discipline and started to try and play like them with short passes and constant movement. It just wasn't us and they came back into the game drawing level. Minutes later they got a third and our heads dropped although with minutes later Cardiff City's George Edwards had a chance on goal when he was rugby tackled by the Portuguese defender and all we got was a free kick. I remember Mal Griffiths ran up to take it and picked it up and dived down for a try in disgust of the decision. At this point the game erupted into a free-for-all between players and as George Edwards and myself were running off the crowd started to chase us towards the dressing room. Later that evening the Welsh FA reprimanded us over our behaviour, and I knew then that some of these selectors had no place in the game. My night was completed when we went to a casino and I lost a few quid on Roulette.

The next day the Welsh team found themselves en route for Belgium via Madrid. Again weather was bad and the plane was diverted to Oporto where it refuelled and headed for Brussels. Again it was a terrible flight that certainly put the players on edge. The team checked into a hotel in the city and Trevor took the opportunity of phoning Louise to let her know how he was doing and how things were back home. Changes were made due to injuries for the Belgium game as Griffiths, Lowrie, Sherwood, Paul and Williams were all out. Wales lost the game at the Liege Sclessian Stadium 3-1, again with Trevor getting the goal, but once again the standard of the refereeing caused great disgust among the Welsh players. They were also disgusted by the attitude of the Belgium team, who again seemed to resort to any illegal tactic that gave them a win. Trevor was battered and bruised but never once retaliated to their provocation. As he put it later in life: 'I was wearing the dragon of Wales so I could not lose my temper.'

That night Trevor smiled to himself as the selectors and their wives enjoyed the hospitality of the Belgium dignitaries. The players were moved to a nearby room where they were allowed a couple of pints, though they really just wanted to go home.

The team left Liege the following day and arrived in Berne, Switzerland, with the walking wounded growing as they prepared for the game at the Berne Stadium. There was a meeting before the game for the officials and Wales, in no uncertain terms, told their hosts they would not be playing with a ball that was not regulation size or that was under-inflated. Trevor recalled:

An hour before kick-off the referee came into the dressing room with the ball, and it was not only smaller but it was soft like a pudding. We refused to play the game and with minutes to go we were still arguing over it. In the end the Welsh FA relented and gave in, so we played. As the game went on the ball got worse and even though we complained the ref did nothing. In the end we lost 4-0. I was glad to get home to my family, but I did learn a few things on that tour, especially how the Welsh FA worked.

Trevor continued to become a pivotal member of the Welsh team, gaining two more caps against England and Scotland late in 1949. With thoughts still on the tour and the treatment of the team, Trevor was thrilled to be selected to play Belgium at Ninian Park in the November of 1949. Many of the Welsh players felt that they owed the Belgians one for their poor sportsmanship during their last encounter.

Ninian Park was full to the rafters as 32,000 fans watched Wales play out of their skin. The game was over by half-time as Wales were 4-0 up with goals from Roy Clarke, Roy Paul, and two from Trevor. He recalled the effect his performance had on the Belgium and Anderlecht 'keeper, Henri Meert:

> I went on the rampage in the Belgium penalty area. I stormed around looking menacing, and wherever the Belgian 'keeper Meert gathered the ball, I went for him like a terrier going for a postman. It was fair intimidation but it broke his spirit. Twice he was looking for me when he should have been looking for the ball.' Trevor ended the game with his first hat-trick as Wales went out winners 5-1.

The Welsh fans had to wait until the spring of 1950 before they could cheer on their team again. The match would be against Northern Ireland at Wrexham's Racecourse ground. The game marked the debut of one of the country's greatest footballers – John Charles. At eighteen years and seventy-one days old, the Swansea boy became the youngest player to wear the red jersey. It was a record that stood for forty-one years until Manchester United's Ryan Giggs gained his first cap for Wales against Germany in 1991. Charles was making a name for himself as a striker with Leeds United, but the selectors picked him to play centre half against the Irish as it was a position he was certainly comfortable with. Trevor knew John well and when John was on the ground staff at Swansea he would clean Trevor and Roy Paul's boots. John's brother Mel explained how thrilled he was to be in the side with them both:

> John idolized both Trevor and Roy. He cleaned their boots and he never forgot how kind they were to him when he was a

youngster coming through the ranks. When he was picked for Wales he could not believe he would be sharing the same dressing room and pitch with them; he was overjoyed.

The game ended 0-0 and by all accounts it was a dire game. The *South Wales Echo* said, 'To call it a poor game would be unkind. It was worse than that.' Trevor never really had a kick, although John Charles did enough to warrant a second cap. Trevor spoke at length to John about his own international debut and what a disappointment it was to him. But he reassured the big centre half that he would be ok.

Trevor's time at Aston Villa appeared to be coming to an end as rumours filled the papers with stories of clubs interested in the young striker. The pressure was growing on him and another disappointing game for Wales did not help matters – they lost at home to Scotland 3-1 in the October of 1950. Weeks after that game Trevor signed for Sunderland and became the most expensive footballer in world football. Days after his signature he turned out for Wales against England at Sunderland's Roker Park. The reception he got from the Sunderland fans in the crowd was incredible as they saw their new signing turning out for what was the opposition. As always England fielded a very strong team that included Jackie Milburn, Leslie Compton, Tom Finney, and Wilf Mannion. England won the game 4-2 with Trevor scoring both Welsh goals in the process. Trevor was overjoyed to have at least showed the Sunderland fans what he could do, even if Wales had struggled. With his club football secured, Trevor went from strength to strength with both Sunderland and Wales, dominating the centre forward position. Recording seven goals in his next nine internationals, including two in Wales, he saw his first ever game at Wembley, where they lost 5-2. The game saw a 93,000 crowd on a Wednesday afternoon and gate receipts topped £44,000. The match was well remembered by Trevor's old foe Billy Wright who said of his encounter with the Welshman, 'It was the first time that I had played at centre half and I could not have asked for a tougher opponent than Trevor Ford.'

The following spring would see Wales play Northern Ireland in Belfast as part of the Home Internationals. John Charles again was scoring regularly for Leeds United in the centre forward position. Charles was swiftly becoming one of the game's hottest properties, with many clubs from home and abroad charting his progress. The Welsh selectors could not ignore this, so with Trevor at number nine they picked Charles to play alongside him at inside right. Making their debuts that day were more Swansea boys in the shape of Derrick Sullivan, Terry Medwin and Harry Griffiths. Wales were superb that day with Charles and Ford unstoppable. Wales ran out 3-2 winners through two Charles goals and one from Trevor. The way the two played certainly made the Welsh selectors take notice as they seemed to realize that they may well have a young replacement for Trevor in the future. Wales's optimism was quickly shattered, as they were demolished a month later 6-1 in Paris by France and then 5-2 in Belgrade by Yugoslavia. The only crumb of comfort was Trevor's two goals against the Yugoslavs. Again Trevor was a wanted man in the domestic transfer market as he signed for Cardiff City. Injury forced him to miss the next few internationals but John Charles certainly enhanced his case for the number nine shirt in Trevor's absence, scoring three goals in four internationals. Trevor returned to the Welsh side as a Cardiff City player in May 1954 with a tough away game against Austria in Vienna. Trevor would be partnered up front by another young forward from Arsenal, Derrick Tapscott, who would be making his debut. John Charles was moved to centre half and Wales welcomed Tottenham Hotspur winger and Swansea lad Cliff Jones into the side for his debut. Cliff recalls the game:

> The Austrians had qualified for the 1954 World Cup and were a good side. It was my debut along with a few others. I was nineteen years of age and I looked around the dressing room and there was Trevor, Roy Paul, and Ronnie Burgess. I couldn't believe I was playing with these lads. I remember Wales's selectors picked the team, but ex-player Wally Barnes was given the duty of being the manager. Wally said to Trevor, 'Listen Trevor, this is continental football. Don't touch the 'keeper as you can't do it here.' Trevor nodded. We kicked off and Roy Paul put a lovely cross into the box, and Trevor hit the 'keeper so hard he flew into the net. The crowd went mental, running towards the pitch to try and get to Trevor, but he just got on with his game. The

ref came over but he just said that he did not understand. At half-time Wally Barnes was furious and said to him, 'What the bloody hell did you do?' Trevor responded with, 'I never touched him.' We all fell about laughing. We lost the game 2-0, but I will always remember how good to me Trevor was.

Another barren spell in front of goal would see Trevor move to inside right to make way for the emerging John Charles at number nine. The move hurt Trevor, but club football showed you were only as good as your last game, and he had gone five internationals without scoring. Welsh international and Tottenham Hotspur player Terry Medwin remembers those times:

> Trevor was always a shoe-in for the centre forward role, but at that time he had Derrick Tapscott and John Charles playing well for club and country. Trevor was invaluable to the team. I know he had his problems at some clubs but he would always give advice and help players like John and Derrick, even though they were supposed to be rivals. All Trevor wanted was for Wales to do well.

As October 1955 came to an end Wales faced the old foe England at Ninian Park. The squad reported to the Angel Hotel in Cardiff on the eve of the game. Cardiff City and Wales captain Alf Sherwood had been given instructions to take control as manager as Wally Barnes had left to take up a job with the BBC. Sherwood actually had a pre-match tactical talk with the players, something Trevor had not witnessed in a Wales set-up before. Sherwood placed Trevor up front with Derrick Tapscott and moved Charles to centre half. Sherwood took responsibility for danger man Stanley Matthews while giving Roy Paul the task of looking after Don Revie. The team would mark man-to-man, which freed up the forwards to cause problems – Trevor would have his own battle with Billy Wright. Sherwood's mantra for the game was 'chase until you drop'. There were 55,000 fans packed into Ninian Park to see if Wales could beat England for the first time in seventeen years. The opening minutes were a tense affair as both sides battled for possession. With fifteen minutes on the clock Trevor got on the end of a Tapscott ball that just went over the bar. Wales started to get on top and on thirty-eight minutes the ball fell to young Derrick

Tapscott and he drilled it home to put Wales 1-0 up. The whole of Ninian Park shook to the rafters as the fans screamed with delight. With England having no time to recover, Roy Paul went down the line and crossed into the centre where Trevor, closely followed by Billy Wright, was running in. Behind them, Cliff Jones ghosted in to head the ball into the England net for 2-0. Again the place erupted amid scenes never witnessed at Ninian Park. Cliff Jones recalls the goal:

> Roy Paul went down the line and I just ran after it. As the ball came across I shouted for Trevor to leave it, which he did, and I just headed it in. When it went in he picked me up and shouted, 'We're going to do it.' The goal tells you everything about Trevor. He was the more experienced player and I was having only my second game, yet I shouted for him to leave it and he did. Many people thought he was a selfish player who only cared about himself, but this proves he was only interested in what was best for Wales.

Half-time could not come soon enough for England and in particular Stanley Matthews, who was not given a kick by Alf Sherwood in the first half. In the second England pulled a goal back through a John Charles own goal, but Wales fought and stuck in. Things seemed to have gone against the men in red when Roy Paul was injured and had to go off, leaving them down to ten men, but they held out for the final whistle and a 2-1 win. The place erupted as Welsh players hugged each other. The dressing room was chaos as the Welsh players sang and danced with jubilation. The celebrations carried on into the night at the Park Hotel in Cardiff. However, Wales could not capitalize on the win as they lost 2-0 away to Scotland and drew 1-1 with Northern Ireland. The results meant that the Home Internationals were shared among the four Home Countries.

Sandwiched in between these games was a second encounter with the Austrians. The game was a spitefully tough game that started when Derrick Tapscott shoulder-charged the Austrian 'keeper Bruno Englemier. Trevor also put himself about in the game, which this lead to the Austrians taking no prisoners when tackling the Welsh. One victim was defender Mel Charles, who was carried off injured with stud marks down his leg. It was a brutal affair. Wales lost 2-1. The *Western Mail* called the game 'a disgrace to football' and singled out Ford and Tapscott, saying that they 'behaved like spoilt stars'. Wales opened the 1956/57 campaign with a new manager in the shape of Manchester United number two Jimmy Murphy. Born in the Rhondda, Murphy played for West Bromwich Albion and earned twenty-two Welsh caps. Murphy's first game was at home against Scotland at Ninian Park. Wales should have won the game but the 60,000 inside Ninian that day saw Wales let a 2-0 lead with goals from Trevor and Terry Medwin slip through their grasp for the game to end 2-2. Trevor received more stick in the press, claiming that he could have had a hat-trick. The *Western Mail* reported, 'How often I wished during this game that Wales had two John Charles. One to make and the other to take the chances.'

With the release of Trevor's book and his subsequent ban, this would turn out to be his last game in the red shirt of Wales, and although his ban was overturned months later, he did not feature in Murphy's future plans. Trevor had played thirty-eight times for his country and scored twenty-three goals, making him the highest goalscorer for Wales along with Ivor Allchurch, who scored twenty-three in sixty-eight games (until 31 March 1993 when Liverpool's Ian Rush broke the record with a goal against Belgium – Rush finished his Wales career with twenty-eight goals in seventy-three internationals). Trevor was devastated not to be picked for his country. His record stood above anyone's but it was plain to see that the Welsh FA and Jimmy Murphy rested all their future hopes on John Charles. Trevor argued that he had done nothing wrong in the Welsh shirt and his book certainly never aimed criticism at the Welsh team, but it fell upon deaf ears.

Wales entered the 1957/58 season knowing that they could qualify for the forthcoming World Cup in Sweden. They did qualify along with all the other hosts nations and with Trevor's ban now rescinded – he was scoring goals regularly over in Holland for PSV Eindhoven – he felt that maybe he had a chance to go. He realized that he would not be number nine as that was now quite rightly John Charles's position, but as they would be taking a squad he thought he had a chance, even though he was thirty-five years old. Forty players were put on a list for the Welsh squad but there was no place for Trevor. No disrespect meant to any of those players, but the forty included non-league players, Welsh league players and players from the forth and third division of English football – players who could not hold a candle to one of the country's greatest players. The press started to talk about Trevor going to the World Cup but the Welsh FA told them that he had burnt his bridges with them – there would be no place for somebody who admits to taking under-the-counter payments in football. The council members of the Welsh FA at the time were lay preachers and, in their own eyes, pillars of society. They had enough of his image and did not like the fact that he would not give them the respect they felt they deserved. They felt that the scandal in the press surrounding him was something they could do without; they wanted players who would be good for the image of Wales and who would toe the line.

Wales went on to Sweden and took the tournament in their stride, drawing 1-1 with Hungary then 1-1 with Mexico, and 0-0 with hosts Sweden before beating Hungary 2-1 in a playoff that guaranteed them a quarter-final date with Brazil. The Brazil game was a game too far for the battered and bruised John Charles who, as Wales' best-known player, was taking supreme punishment from opposing defenders. Charles missed the game through injury and the Welsh selectors suddenly realized the squad was lacking centre forwards. Manchester United's Colin Webster was thrown in and gave a valiant display, but he was not the same type of forward as Tapscott or Ford. Wales were beaten 1-0 by Brazil with a goal from a certain seventeen-year-old called Pelé. Looking back at the chances Wales had in the game, it was easy for press and fans to think maybe Trevor should have gone. Many players could also not understand the Welsh FA's thinking. Cliff Jones remembered:

> I have no doubt that Trevor Ford should've gone to the World Cup. He would've got goals anywhere. The Welsh FA never put the team first. I they had they would of taken him. They made up their minds ages ago. They never even saw him play in Holland to see how he was getting on. Trevor was a clever footballer; he read the game and was skilful. He was a rascal but a proud Welshman.

Terry Medwin's opinion was that, 'Without doubt he should have gone along with Derrick Tapscott who was not taken.' Tapscott alleged in later life that while playing for Arsenal he was approached by a Welsh selector and Cardiff City director and told 'if you sign for Cardiff City you can go to the World Cup'. Tapscott refused and subsequently found himself left out of the World Cup squad. Team member Colin Baker recalled:

> It was scandalous. We only really had John up front and they never thought 'what if he gets injured?' They were so short-sighted. I was a surprise choice to go and I could not believe Trevor was not included. It was a poor decision not made on football grounds but pettiness by the Welsh FA. I think it cost us in the end.

Mel Charles also remember the decision:

> Myself and John were aghast when Trevor was not even mentioned about going. I know Trevor made things difficult for himself at times, but what he said in his book was true: Everyone was getting payments here and there. I don't understand what it had to do with Wales.' Trevor said in later life that he wished he had released the book after the World Cup – that way he would have gone – but in all honesty I don't think he thought they would qualify. He said, 'I would've done well in Sweden. I had altered my game whilst playing in Holland and I was playing teams from Holland Spain and Italy so I could of past on my experience to the other lads.'

He admitted the whole tournament was painful for him to watch and a little bit of his love for the game disappeared.

12

The Forgotten Man

With the hurt and disappointment of the World Cup behind him, Trevor returned from his customary foreign holiday with his family to life in the Netherlands. He and Louise, along with youngest son Martyn, found comfort in the affection shown to them by the local Eindhoven community. Trevor's oldest son David continued his studies at boarding school in Cardiff. Whereas before young David would be kept abreast of how his dad was doing in Holland by one of the housemasters, things were certainly different now, with both of them struggling to find any sort of report or news story involving Trevor at all. There was another managerial change at the club as George Hardwick moved on to concentrate on the Netherland's national side. Hardwick's replacement was Cees Van Dijcke. Van Dijcke had been a full-back with his hometown club Feyenord during the 1920s where he amassed over 250 competitive games. He also represented the Netherlands three times. After his playing career he became a trainer at various Dutch teams such as Feyenord, Noad, and Xerxes. The job was his first in management.

The season felt different for Trevor; he was still struggling with the constant ankle problem that had, to a certain extent, blighted some of his career, and he knew that the season would be a bit of a struggle in terms of getting games behind him. He had altered his game since playing with PSV and he was now playing a bit deeper in attack. His new position meant he could hold the ball up and bring the midfielders into play more instead of charging towards the 'keeper like he used to; in fact the physical side of his game was certainly diminishing. He still had a bit of pace about him and he never lost that knack of being in the right place at the right time. What was different was trying to block out the fact that he was no longer a Welsh international footballer. He never gave up hope and deep down he hoped a good season might get him noticed again. He knew it was a long shot but that's what he would have loved. Being a proud person he knew he would never beg the Welsh FA to reconsider; all he said on the matter when asked was 'I am still available.'

New manager Van Dijcke had the same training methods as the other managers who had gone before him, and there was real emphasis on ball control and passing and moving. Trevor's instincts into the season ahead proved right as he struggled with only a handful of games during the 1958/59 season. His ankle was a constant problem, and although an operation to remove some bone seemed to do the trick for a while, he knew deep down that he may have to forget this season in readiness for the next. He was just as popular with the fans and he and Louise were still treated like royalty wherever they went around Eindhoven. At the end of the season he had played only ten games and scored three goals in the process as PSV finished the season in tenth place, way behind winners Sparta Rotterdam.

When the season ended it was plain to see that Louise was starting to get homesick. She would spend weekends back in Wales whenever she could and she was still not comfortable with young David being so far away from the rest of the family. Something had to give and in the summer of 1959 Trevor and Louise decided that it would be better if Louise moved back to Cardiff with Martyn. Trevor had a year left on his contract and he intended to see it out. He decided that he would come home more in between games, and although that would put pressure on him, he knew it was best for his family, as he wanted to be a part of his boys' lives. His friend Stan Stennett came over to Eindhoven to keep him company before the new season started and he spent hours with Stan talking about what the future would hold for him and whether he would get another club after his stint in Holland. They also talked about the possibility of Trevor starting a business, maybe car related, in the future. Although Trevor had a some money in the bank, he knew he would have to sort something out for the future. With Stan back in the UK, Trevor concentrated on the new season and unbelievably PSV started a new season with another coach, this time an old face from his first season at the club – Yugoslavian Ljubiša Broćić. The two got on really well and Trevor was keen to see him back at the club. Although committed to the cause as always, Trevor knew deep down that this would be his last in Dutch football. He passed the news on to the board and they pleaded with him to reconsider at the end of the season. Popular as ever with the PSV fans, they also tried to change his mind about staying and poor old Trevor could not go to dinner or out shopping without being approached and asked to stay. He loved having their support and deep down he needed to feel wanted, especially as his family was in another country. The distance between them hit home when on arrival at Heathrow for one visit, he was greeted by Louise, David and Martyn. David recalls the incident:

> We were waiting for Dad to come off the aeroplane and when he did I remember shaking his hand and saying "Hello sir". I think looking back it really upset him. Although I would have been about nine he hated the fact that he was a stranger to me. It was things like that which made him want to come home.

The 1959/60 season started well for Trevor as he scored one of the goals in a 2-0 victory away at Fortuna. A succession of five draws followed with Trevor getting a last-minute equalizer against rivals Feyenord to earn the club a point. Although results were inconsistent, Trevor was pleased that he was staying fit for games and playing regularly. This was important as he started to have thoughts that maybe he could still do a job back in the Football League when he returned to the UK. Trevor made sure he commuted home on a regular basis and the directors at PSV were helpful in giving him time off so he could stay in the UK for longer. They had also made sure that he never really had to do much for the Philips Corporation at all in his time at the club; all he really did was have his photo taken for product launches or appear at trade shows. Over the whole four years he knew that they had been good to him and he would never forget it. The season turned out to be one of inconsistency for PSV and that probably summed up the club during his time there. They finished the season in tenth position again with Trevor netting eight goals in twenty-five games. Trevor's time in the Netherlands, although forced due to his ban, had turned out to be one of the happiest in his career. He had met and made friends forever at the club. He felt a better player and later in life he remarked that he should have gone abroad earlier to benefit from European football. PSV were in the initial stages of professional football when he joined and there was certainly no hint of the successful European side they would become. There was pressure on him to deliver and that's what he did, scoring twenty-one goals in fifty-three games for the club. Many were sad to see Trevor leave the club and even today he is well remembered. Dutch journalist and PSV Eindhoven historian Frans Claes has nothing but admiration for the Welshman:

> Trevor Ford is still loved by the PSV fans. He was our first big foreign signing. Many older fans talk about his bravery and skill on the pitch and many talk about the gentleman he was off the pitch. When he signed we could not believe it. We knew that there was some scandal involved in him coming but he was nothing but professional when he pulled on the shirt. I feel it was Wales and British football's loss and our gain when he came here. He often came back to see the club and he was always given a rapturous welcome. Fans put him up there with some of the greats the club has had like Ruud Gullit, Ronald Koeman, Ruud Van Nistelrooy, Ronaldo, and Romario. That's how great he was.

With Trevor's impending move he thought about whether clubs would come in for him. He had put feelers out when ever he visited home and there was talk of a few clubs being interested, but now, aged thirty-seven, he needed concrete offers and as yet there was nothing. He thought that maybe it was time to hang up the boots. Unfortunately for Trevor the football world had, to a certain extent, forgotten him. His age and reputation certainly did not help and those days of record-breaking transfers and playing in front of packed houses at some of the best stadiums in Britain were long gone.

While home in Cardiff, Trevor decided to set up his own garage in the Whitchurch area of the city. He knew the business inside and out from his days at Sunderland, and although Cardiff City were not interested in him anymore, the local people of Cardiff were, and they were more than happy to buy a car off Trevor Ford. People trusted him and they also had that reassurance that he was still a well-known name who had a reputation to keep. The garage meant long hours for Trevor but he loved it and business went from strength to strength. Trevor felt relaxed and happy that he had his family around him once again. The move to Cardiff also coincided with young David coming out of boarding school and going into the local secondary modern. Both Trevor and Louise were happy to have him home now but the children's education was important to both of them and they were always on the lookout for any means to further the boys in life.

With thoughts of getting back into football slipping away, he suddenly got a call from ex-Swansea teammate and Welsh international Billy Lucas, who was now manager of Newport County, currently in the Third Division of the Football League. Lucas had been a tough wing-half who played for Wolverhampton Wanderers, Swindon Town, Swansea Town, and Newport County, where he had been player-manager since 1953. Lucas had first became aware of Trevor while at Swansea and he thought that maybe the striker would turn out for his club and add a bit of experience. Trevor was flattered with the enquiry, and although there had been rumours about different teams' interest in his services, this was a firm offer from a club just up the road. Trevor met Lucas and the two men thrashed out a deal. PSV still had Trevor's registration so a fee of £1,000 was agreed between the two clubs for Trevor to move. Trevor was thrilled with the news. He still had a few injury problems but to play again, and for a Welsh club, was something he could only have dreamed about this late in his career. Besides Lucas there were a few old faces in the side that he recognized, such as Scots winger John McSeveney, who had been at Sunderland and Cardiff City with Trevor. He also recognised Cec Dixon, who had been the player that stepped in for Trevor at Cardiff City when he refused to play at inside left against Birmingham City.

Although Trevor signed in the June of 1960 his injuries were a cause for concern and he wasn't able to his debut until October away against Brentford. Newport County won 4-2 but Trevor found it hard getting back to the pace of the game. He certainly never shirked away from tough challenges but, now in his late thirties, he couldn't shake them off like he could in his younger days. Trevor now had a run in the side, but the goals seemed elusive. Newport lost 4-1 away at Shrewsbury Town in the FA Cup and a 0-0 draw with Torquay followed before Trevor found the net in a 3-3 friendly at Wrexham's racecourse ground. As Trevor trudged off the pitch he couldn't help thinking about all the times he had played for Wales at this ground, and there was part of him that thought maybe this was going to be tougher game than he had first thought. Trevor scored his first league goal in the December as Newport County beat Chesterfield 5-1. He followed that goal up with a consolation goal for Newport as they went down 4-1 to Bury. Trevor's ankle and knee were becoming a problem, especially after games. He played in the 3-2 victory away at Reading but then missed the next two games with injury. Trevor came back at the start of 1961 as Newport lost 4-2 away at Southend United and 3-0 at Bristol City.

Lifelong Bristol City supporter Alan Mead remembers Ford playing at Ashton Gate:

> I was amazed to see him turning out for Newport County. He had always been a big star in football and to see him in his late thirties playing in the lower divisions was a real shame. You could tell he still had skill, but a player of Ford's calibre should have just retired at the top. I particularly remember people around us asking if it was Trevor Ford. Many people thought he retired after Cardiff City; I never knew he went to Holland to play.

Trevor's last league goal was in the 3-1 home defeat against Queens Park Rangers at the end of January. He was obviously in pain and then missed the next six games.

Trevor knew that his days as a footballer were finished once and for all. He was dropping into the reserves to try and gain some fitness but ending his career in the Welsh League was something he did not want to do. Trevor thought long and hard and decided to leave the club. Billy Lucas put out a statement to the press: 'We have parted company with Trevor Ford due to his disinclination to play in the reserves. It's been unfortunate he has been dogged by injuries since returning from Holland. We have finished up on friendly terms.' Trevor told the press that he had no other options, but wouldn't mind a crack at management. Unfortunately, the phone never rang.

Although Trevor was only with the club a few months, he certainly made an impression on some of the players. Goalkeeper Len Weare recalls:

> When I was younger at Wolves I saw Trevor whack goalkeeper Bert Williams Trevor put him in the net with the ball before he had even landed. I don't think Bert ever recovered. Trevor was a tough guy. He would turn up for training in a big Cadillac. It was like a bus. They had to widen the gates so he could get it in. He was tight though. A few of us smoked and in those days you offered your cigarettes around. Trevor only ever had one left when it was his turn.

Inside forward Jimmy Singer also remembers him:

> Trevor Ford was a legend. He used to pick me up every morning. I was only a scruffy boy from Cefn Hengoed and Fordy would turn up in this big Cadillac. A hell of a boy he was remembered 'Half back Les Riggs'. Trevor was quite the star. You should have seen his overcoats and the size of his car.

Ollie Burton recalls:

> Playing up front with Trevor was an experience. I could watch him all day, he was fantastic.

Suddenly out of the blue Trevor was thrown a lifeline with a job offer of work in Central London at a prestige garage. The offer was good with decent money and a flat provided. He talked things over with Louise and they decided that he would work Monday to Friday and come home for the weekends. With the move Trevor decided to sell his garage in Cardiff, and although he was in trouble with injuries he still agreed when a colleague at the garage asked him to turn out for local non-league side Romford, who were in the Southern League at the time. Local Supporter Harry Wilks remembers Trevor:

> It was a great move on our part. Trevor came to the club and was really popular. We knew it was only going to be for a few games but he was never the big-time Charlie with us all. He would be helpful and keep the lads busy for hours with his stories about the game. I don't think he was that keen on playing towards the end of his time with us due to old injuries, even though he still got a couple of goals for us, but he loved the training.

Trevor would spend some weekday evenings watching some of the London clubs and he would invariably meet up with ex-players after the game for a drink. Louise would also come up to London with the boys and stay weekends at the flat, and although it was great that they were together Trevor knew in his heart of hearts that this was not a long-term arrangement as he certainly did not want to move to London and make this permanent.

After a couple of years in the capital, Trevor received another offer of work from a very old friend, W. S. Martin, his old director at Sunderland. He asked if he would be interested in working for him back up north. The job was selling cars, which by now Trevor was a natural at, but this time it would need all the family to move back to the North East. David was now at a boarding school in the Brecon Beacons and very happy, so the family moved back to Sunderland to take up the offer. Trevor loved the North East and would have liked to have stayed there if things had worked out at Roker Park. Again Trevor was successful in his role of managing the garages that Martin owned. The two men had always got on together and they both trusted each other implicitly. There was never any bad blood towards Trevor and the Sunderland public, despite the after-effects of his book and the consequent investigation of the club, which almost brought it to its knees. Trevor was always welcomed with open arms by the Roker Park faithful if he attended any game. Trevor enjoyed the contact with ex-footballers, many of them ones he had had real battles with in the past – seeing them again brought out a mutual respect between both parties. Although he had finished relatively early, and certainly under a cloud, he could still call in the odd favour and this he did when son David asked him if he could maybe get him a trial at a club.

David takes up the story:

I must have been around thirteen or fourteen years of age and was in a boarding school in Brecon. The school was a rugby school and although I enjoyed the game my real love was football and I would play whenever I got the chance with my other boarders. I knew I would never really get an opportunity for a trial while I was at the school so I asked Dad if he could get me a trial at a club. Dad thought long and hard and after a pause he said leave it to me. Typical of the way in which he always wanted myself and Martyn to have the best, he rang his old friend Matt Busby at Manchester United and days later I was invited to go to the Cliff training ground in Salford for the week in half-term. I couldn't believe it but that was Dad all over. He came down from Sunderland and picked me up to take me to Manchester. In the car he told me to do as I was told, listen and, above all, do my best. At the end of the week United were playing Sunderland at Roker Park and he had arranged, whatever the result of my trial, for me to travel with the first team up to the North East where he would meet me. I was thrilled.

The week was fantastic: I trained with other trialists and took part in a trialist's game. I then trained along with the youth team and met the first team where I was surrounded by the likes of a young George Best, Bobby Charlton, Tony Dunne, Dennis Law, Bill Folkes, Johnny Giles and Captain Noel Cantwell. The first team had just won the FA Cup, beating Leicester City 3-1. At the end of the week the coaches gave no indication of how I had done, but to be honest I was just in my element being with these players and hearing their stories of my Dad and what a player he had been. I remember feeling immensely proud of him as people like Bobby Charlton and Matt Busby told me that he was one of the greats. Even at fourteen years of age I knew that these men were talking from the heart.

When we arrived at Roker Park I met up with Dad and we watched the game in which Sunderland won 1-0. After the game Dad was in discussions with Matt Busby for what seemed like ages as I waited in the car. We eventually left for home and Dad told me that United thought that I was not up to scratch. I was disappointed but I had a great week and thought about going back to school.

Years later Dad told me that United had been interested in giving me an apprenticeship when I turned sixteen but Dad had told them that I would be doing nothing until I left school and finished my education. In hindsight he was right: I wasn't distraught at the news that United did not want me and I had no hunger to contact any other clubs for a trial. I just thought well that was that. There are probably loads of reasons why Dad did not tell me that day in the car, the main ones I feel are that he wanted me to make something of myself. An education was really important to him and Mum. I also think that he knew I had no burning desire to be a footballer, just an idea of whether I could do it, and I think he thought that although football had moved on since his day, he just did not want me being any part of the game that had treated him like it had.'

Things were going well for Trevor at the car dealership and the family were loving life in the north-east of England. David, who was now seventeen, had relocated to Sunderland with his job at Lloyds Bank, and he and Trevor became closer, going to watch Sunderland whenever they could. But unfortunately a year after David's move Trevor's mother became ill and the family moved back to Swansea. Trevor's relationship with W. S. Martin became strained as the businessman did not want him to leave, but the pull of south Wales was too much for Trevor and found a job selling prestige cars for Julian Hodge in Cardiff. Being an ex-sportsman made it easier for Trevor to make sales, as they were intrigued to find out what he had been up to and they felt they could trust him.

The family were again happy when David relocated back to south Wales with his job and was there to support his parents. As with Sunderland, David and Trevor spent a lot of time together mainly watching Trevor's other great love, cricket .The pair would often spend the day watching Glamorgan and Trevor even turned out for the team's reserves now and then. It was one such August day in 1968 when Trevor and David went to see Glamorgan play Nottinghamshire at the St Helens ground in Swansea. As the pair sat down to watch the day's events, Nottinghamshire captain

Gary Sobers won the toss and chose to bat first. During the lunch interval Glamorgan fast bowler Ossie Wheatley reported an injury. Glamorgan had no twelfth man so a call went up for help. David takes up the story:

> Officials were running around not knowing what to do when one of the club men noticed Dad and asked him if he could step in until a replacement could be found. Dad said, 'Give me some kit and I will play.' Glamorgan accepted and Dad went out in the field at mid-off for an hour before Alan Rees arrived from home to relieve him as twelfth man. Many people think Dad was fielding when Gary Sobers famously hit six sixes. Dad fielded from 2 p.m. until 3 p.m., but Sobers started his famous feat at 5 p.m. when me and Dad were back in the stands. I remember Dad giving poor Glamorgan bowler Malcolm Nash plenty of stick after the game.

Being back in Wales also gave Trevor the chance to meet up with his old mate Stan Stennett and even dust off the old football boots to play for Stan's celebrity football team across Wales and the South West, raising money for local charities. Trevor loved these games and would be as professional as ever, making sure he gave 100 per cent no matter whom his opposition was.

Unfortunately, things came to an abrupt halt in 1969 when, while travelling from Cardiff to Swansea, Trevor had a car accident in Bridgend. David recalls that fateful night:

> I was staying with Dad in the Cardiff flat he had above his old garage. Dad was working for Julian Hodge and was getting ready to leave home for Swansea. He asked me if I wanted to come home with him for the evening but I declined and stayed in the flat. We hugged and said goodbye to each other. Later on in the evening it came over the radio that ex-Welsh footballer Trevor Ford had been rushed to hospital after a car accident in Bridgend. Mum contacted me and told me she was at the hospital. Dad was unconscious in intensive care with various broken bones, cracked ribs and a punctured lung.
>
> The reports of the accident were sketchy but it appeared a car was overtaking and hit Dad's car. I froze when I saw Dad's car

at the compound, as the whole of the passenger side was caved in as it took most of the impact. I realized I would not be here today if I had accepted that lift. Dad eventually pulled through and he was showered with good luck cards from supporters of Wales and all the clubs he had played for during his career. Mum got real comfort from reading the messages to him and he never forgot all those kind words people showered on him. Dad eventually left hospital after a couple of months and went home to recuperate. After a couple of weeks of rest he was ready to return to work.

Trevor returned to work and still continued to play the odd celebrity match for Stan's football team. Even though Trevor was in his fifties, he was still fit and active apart from the odd knee trouble; in fact the doctors told him that it was his fitness that probably saved his life in the car crash all those years ago. Life was settling down. David and Martyn were carving out their own careers and life was good for him and Louise.

Trevor was enjoying his time at Julian Hodge but found himself headhunted by a large Mercedes-Benz garage in Gorsiegnon, Swansea, called Nayland Motors. Trevor was flattered by their offer and to a certain extent it probably inflated his ego a bit – there was more money involved and various other packages were offered. After much deliberation, Trevor accepted their offer and left Julian Hodge. However, after several years' service Trevor was asked into the office and told he was being let go. He had signed no contract with the company when he joined and, naively, he only had a handshake as a guarantee. He left with virtually nothing. At sixty years of age he suddenly found himself on the scrapheap. The frustration of the whole affair was very difficult for him to handle. He knew he probably should not have left Julian Hodge and he knew it was silly to have just relied on a handshake, but he took people at their word, which was his ultimate downfall. He mulled over things in his head and knew that he would have never have made the same mistake if this was a football contract. The realisation really stuck with him and the resulting redundancy would see him never work again.

13

Back from the Cold

Although Trevor found himself with no job at sixty, he continued to be optimistic. Although Trevor had earnt good money over the years, now spare cash was hard to come by. Feeling philosophical, Trevor decided they would sell their house in Swansea and live in the flat they owned near the Gower. Trevor also decided he would sell some of his football memorabilia, such as Welsh caps international shirts that he had worn and swapped with various players as well as a gold watch given to him by a club director, to bring in some money. He knew it was the right thing to do but being the type of man he was, he struggled with the knowledge that he couldn't give Louise all the nice things she was used to, even though most of the time she never asked for anything. What helped him most over this period was the affection some of his ex-players showed him. He would be invited to various football dinners where he would mix with some of his old adversaries and to be back in that world again made him feel invincible. Trevor's son David went with him on many of these occasions:

> Looking back, those long drives me and Dad had on the way to various functions gave me the opportunity to talk to him about his career and to a certain extent fill in some holes that I had growing up. He loved the game even though some parts of it had treated him badly. He never really got over not being picked for the 1958 World Cup and the attitude of the Welsh FA. He had many invites to attend games at Aston Villa, which he did. They really pushed out the red carpet for him, giving him seats

in the directors' box and he loved it when he was introduced to
the crowd and they all cheered his name. Chairman at the time
Doug Ellis was a big fan of Dad's and he always made sure he
sat with him. I think looking back Aston Villa were his happiest
times and probably where he played his best football; the Villa
supporters always told him that when he visited. Sunderland also
invited him to games and he was always welcome at Swansea
and Cardiff City, which he loved.

I will always have this memory of us at a large football do at
the Piccadilly Hotel in Manchester. People paid £25 a head for
a ticket, which was a lot in the early 1980s. It was a black-tie
affair and some of British football's greats were at the do, and
most of them were on our table, players like Billy Wright, Tom
Finney, Bobby Charlton, Stanley Matthews – the list was endless.
I just sat back and was amazed by the affection shown to Dad.
There was a queue of people waiting for autographs and that
queue was for Dad. What is more incredible was that in that
queue was George Best and Dennis Law who told him he was
one of the greats. Dad signed George's menu and the Irishman
asked if Dad would dedicate it to his son, Callum. I could see in
Dad's face how happy he was around those fellow players. He
even met Len Shackleton and they shook hands and chatted for a
few minutes, but you could see they were never going to keep in
touch. Looking back those events gave him some pride back and
it showed me how well thought of he was.

By a strange twist of fate in 1986, Stan Stennett's son Ceri joined
the Welsh FA, working with the media and the press. The FA
that Ceri joined was pretty much the same as it had always been
but with his love of Welsh football, Ceri decided to make a few
changes:

My job at the Welsh FA was in charge of the media. The FA
knew that they had to bring their whole operation into modern
times. I was always a big fan of Welsh football and Trevor Ford
was my godfather and somebody I looked up to since I was a
small boy. I loved listening to his stories of games and he owned
a trunk with all his caps and shirts in. Every time my family
visited I would ask if I could see the trunk. He was a wonderful

man. I only really knew how famous he was when his picture popped up in my Charles Buchan football book whilst playing for Aston Villa. In those early days of my job the Welsh FA had all sorts of memorabilia knocking about in boxes all over the offices and they did not know what to do with it, so I decided to see if we could display it and celebrate Welsh football of the past. We now have such a place in Wrexham County Borough Museum. The Welsh FA also seemed to have no contact with any ex-players and if they wanted to see a game they had to write in. So I decided we should find out where they all were and get their addresses on a database and invite them to games rather than get them to ask. Finally we decided to hold regular dinners where we could celebrate a particular player, and of course one of the first was Trevor Ford. I was determined that his efforts for Wales would never be forgotten. He told me that he always wanted to be accepted back by Wales; it showed how deeply hurt he had been.'

Trevor seemed to have had a new lease of life as he continued with retirement. Welsh football legend Alan Curtis remembers seeing him about in Swansea:

Trevor was a good friend of my uncle Roy Paul, who also played for Wales. I would always bump into Trevor at dinners and also around the town. He was suffering a bit with his knee and ankle but I was amazed how fit he looked. He was always immaculately turned out, even in later life. We would talk for ages about modern football and how the Welsh clubs were doing. He was a remarkable man.

As the years went on Trevor's knee problem became more and more aggressive, leaving him unable to walk sometimes. He was also in terrible pain with it, which affected his sleep and everyday life. The family went to see a surgeon and the diagnosis was that he needed a knee replacement immediately but the waiting list to have it done through the NHS was over a year. He could go private but it would cost around £8,000. Trevor was in his late seventies and he certainly didn't have that kind of money lying around. David met with his parents as they tried to find a way to move forward. Suddenly David hit on the idea of asking the Welsh FA if they would pay for the operation. Trevor was reluctant to ask but David and Louise wrote the letter anyway. They never told Ceri Stennett, as they did not want to put him in an awkward position. Weeks later they received a response from the FA saying the request was denied as they did not do that sort of thing. The family were appalled by the news; as for Trevor, well he was mortified that he had gone to ask for help and they had said no. He told David that he had never refused Wales in the whole of his career but even now they could still refuse him. Filled with anger, David wrote to the Professional Footballers Association chairman Gordon Taylor, who replied telling them to get it done and they would pay. Taylor remembers the request:

We have 4,000 members and over 50,000 ex-members; this sort of stuff is what we do. We help players with education and also any ex-player who needs our help. You don't suddenly stop being a PFA member just because you don't play anymore. We are a family and are here to help. It was an honour for me personally to help Trevor Ford. While growing up in Manchester me and my mates were obsessed with playing football and collecting anything to do with the game. We were always hanging around Manchester United's and Manchester City's grounds, hoping to see any player. We also went to hotels where we thought we could find the opposition team for autographs, and that's where Trevor Ford gave me an autograph when he was at Sunderland.

He was a pioneer for justice in the game, very much like his countryman Billy Meredith who was our first chairman in 1907. Meredith spoke out about the maximum wage then and Trevor was the same. In 1957 Trevor's book got the ball rolling for ending the maximum wage in 1963. People like him, Jimmy Hill and George Eastham should always be remembered. Many of today's superstars owe an immense debt to people like Trevor Ford as it took guts to stand up to the Football Authorities and football owners; many didn't and accepted the status quo. Trevor paid the price, being exiled by Wales for the 1958 World Cup in Sweden. He should always be remembered as one of the true greats from British football.'

Trevor received the operation at a cost of £7,904, paid for by the PFA.

The bitterness towards the Welsh FA never really went away for Trevor or the family. Trevor was now seventy-seven years old and as the new millennium arrived he started to get the initial stages of dementia. Looking back at recent surveys involving high-profile players such as West Bromwich Albion's Jeff Astle, who passed away in 2002 after being diagnosed with dementia, there appears to be a real link between heading heavy balls, as players in those days did, and the illness. With Astle's case the coroner Andrew Haigh ruled that extensive damage to his brain was the direct cause of heading footballs in his fifteen-year career. Out of the Astle case came the 'Justice for Jeff' campaign, funding more studies into the connection between the number of ex-players suffering from the illness. According to the Football Association, their findings are still ongoing. Trevor's illness restricted how far away from home he could travel. He would get confused at football dinners, sometimes often forgetting people's names, but with David at his side he still enjoyed going.

The family were dealt another huge blow in 2003 when Louise was diagnosed with terminal cancer. The news had a terrible effect on Trevor and he started to deteriorate quickly. David recalled:

> When Mum was diagnosed he really went downhill fast. I think he knew she would be leaving him and she had always been his rock. The thought of not having her around made him give up.

Later that year Trevor was admitted to the Singleton Hospital in Swansea with breathing difficulties. His dementia had accelerated rapidly and now the family knew the end was in sight.

On 29 May 2003, Trevor lost his fight for life, surrounded by his wife Louise and his two sons, David and Martyn. The news hung like a cloud over British football; players from every era wanted to share their opinion of great man. Sir Tom Finney said, 'I have just heard the news and it's a great shame. Trevor was a gent who was always a formidable opponent.' John Charles told the press, 'I'm so sad. I watched him as a kid and he was my idol. Wales have lost one of the Greats.' George Best: 'I never saw him play but met him on many functions. I was drawn to him as he looked like a superstar. My Dad told me he saw him run the Irish defence ragged at times.'

Welsh forward Ian Rush, who broke Trevor's scoring record recalled:

> He was definitely one of the greatest Welsh players and a wonderful person. It's so sad he's gone. I met him a few times and I remember the night I broke his record against Belgium at Cardiff he came over to me, shook my hand, and said 'well done'. His death is a very sad day for Welsh football.

Trevor's funeral was at Llwynderw parish church and it was packed with family, well-wishers and former colleagues. Stan Stennett gave a warm and emotional speech about his great friend that left everyone in tears. Among the flowers were acknowledgements from all his clubs, as well as the Welsh FA, which he would have loved. Trevor was buried at Oystermouth cemetery, Swansea. A year later his beloved Louise joined him when she passed away in 2004.

For David the loss of his father had been a huge blow, but as the dust settled on the passing of both parents he took great comfort remembering the car trips they had made on the way to various functions, where they had talked about his career endlessly and the hours spent watching cricket together.

David took it upon himself to clear away his father's things and over a period of time found out things about his Dad and his family that he never knew.

> I remember clearing out some of Dad's old papers when I came across a letter from the Salvation Army explaining to Dad that they had tried but failed to trace a women called Doris Simmonds and her son Thomas who may be living in London. I had no idea who these people were but after doing some detection work, and asking Dad's sister Joan, I found out that I had a half-brother called Thomas from my Dad's first marriage. I never knew Dad was married before and the whole thing came as a shock. I was angry with Dad at first but then he at least had tried to find his son Thomas, who would be in his seventies now. That's why

I wanted this in the book. So if he is out there I would love to meet him. Although Dad loved me and Martyn, he obviously never forgot Thomas.

Fast forward to 2014 when, out of the blue, David received a call from a women called Vanessa. She was calling from Surrey and wanted to come to Swansea and meet David as she had some information about David's grandfather, Trevor. Intrigued, David, along with Trevor's sister Joan, met Vanessa in a Swansea hotel.

It appeared that Vanessa's father was David's grandfather, Trevor Ford Snr. Trevor Snr had left Trevor's mother Daisy after meeting a young woman called Carol, who had been one of Trevor Jnr's old girlfriends. Carol tried to end the affair but Trevor Snr followed her to London, divorced Daisy and they married despite a thirty-year age gap, and as a result Vanessa was born. Vanessa had no idea that she was connected to footballer Trevor Ford, but she did remember that, when her father was dying, a big American car pulled up outside the house with a well-dressed man and two other men at his side; they came in to see her father and shut the door on her, leaving her outside. When her father passed away with cancer in 1969 Vanessa cleared out his effects and found a box full of press cuttings and articles all about footballer Trevor Ford. It was then that she realized that her father was also Trevor's father. It appeared he had never stopped following Trevor, even though it was from afar, and he was incredibly proud of what he achieved in the game. Many a time he would go to a game and watch him when he was playing a London club, then after he would just go home. Vanessa remembers how her father would talk about this lad Trevor and his brothers and sister with her mum Carol, and how well they were doing, and now it finally clicked that they were all related. She also told David that her father and his had met now and again when Trevor was in London and also, ironically, that his grandfather had been a talent scout for Arsenal and Wolverhampton Wanderers. David reflects:

This has all been a lot to take in and this book I feel has helped me. Vanessa is a lovely lady and I again wanted this book to be a warts-and-all look at my Dad. Many will criticize him for leaving his son Thomas, but it showed how much he was in love with my mum Louise that they stayed together so long. And obviously my grandfather was in love with Carol as they stayed together for a long time. Meeting Vanessa has also helped me fill in the gaps regarding my own granddad, who I only remember meeting once. I know Dad told me how important he was to him when he was growing up and teaching him football skills, then all of a sudden he never talked about him; even when I asked him he just said he left and changed the subject. I think the two men were very similar; they believed that they made a mistake in their early life, and although that is not a problem today, back then to leave a wife and family was not the done thing, and I believe they both carried that guilt around with them all their lives, and because of the events of the past they tried extra hard with their new families. It was plain to see how loved Vanessa was by her Dad and this was the same for me and my brother Martyn. Maybe that's what drove my Dad on to be the best he could.

From head to toe, on and off the field, he wanted to be somebody, have the best and look the best. Looking back he certainly achieved that, because as a footballer and, above all, a father, he was the best. I am extremely proud to have been Trevor Ford's son. People are so nice when they find out he's my father and it's incredible to listen to their stories of how much joy he gave them when he played. I feel he has not been forgotten by the game and its supporters and I was immensely proud when, in 2015, Swansea City contacted me to tell me they were putting Dad in their hall of fame. To me he was just Dad, and I think it's fitting that he has a place in the history of British football.

Trevor's Record

SWANSEA TOWN	9 GOALS	16 MATCHES	1946–1947
ASTON VILLA	60 GOALS	120 MATCHES	1947–1950
SUNDERLAND	70 GOALS	117 MATCHES	1950–1953
CARDIFF CITY	39 GOALS	96 MATCHES	1953–1956
PSV EINDHOVEN	21 GOALS	53 MATCHES	1957–1960
NEWPORT COUNTY	3 GOALS	8 MATCHES	1960–1961
ROMFORD	2 GOALS	8 MATCHES	1961
WALES	23 GOALS	38 MATCHES	1946–1957

Bibliography

While I have undertaken numerous interviews in researching this book, the following is a list of publications that helped to provide me with some excellent background information:

Adamson, Richard, *Bogota Bandit* (Mainstream Publishing, 1996)

Allen, Robert, *'Billy'. The Biography of Billy Bingham* (Viking, 1986)

Charles, Mel & Colin Leslie, *In the Shadow of a Giant*, (John Blake, 2009)

Crooks, John, *The Official History of the Bluebirds* (Yore Publications, 1992)

Ford, Trevor, *I Lead the Attack* (Stanley Paul, 1957)

Jones, Colin, *Swansea Town & City Football Club* (Cyhoeddwyr Dinefwr, 2012)

Giller, Norman, *Billy Wright: A Hero For All Seasons* (Robson Books, 2002)

Goodyear, Simon, *The Gerry Hitchens Story* (DB Publishing, 2010)

Graham, Bob, *The History of Sunderland AFC 1879–1995* (Wearside Publications, 1995)

Grandin, Terry, *Cardiff City 100 Years of Professional Football* (Vertical Editions, 2010)

Green, Geoffrey, *Soccer in the Fifties* (Ian Allen, 1974)

Harding, John, *Behind the Glory: 100 Years of the PFA* (Breedon Books, 2009)

Hardy, Lance, *Stokoe, Sunderland and '73* (Orion, 2009)

Hayes, Dean P., *Wales. The Complete Who's Who Of Footballers Since 1946* (Sutton Publishing, 2004)

Inglis, Simon, *Soccer in the Dock: A History Of British Football Scandals, 1900–1965* (Collins Willow, 1985)

Jenkins, Geraint, *Proud to be a Swan: The History of Swansea City AFC* (Yllolfa, 2012)

Leighton, James, *Duncan Edwards: The Greatest* (Simon & Schuster, 2012)

Lloyd, Grahame, *C'mon City: 100 Years of the Bluebirds* (Seren, 1999)

Malam, Colin, *The Len Shackleton Story: Clown Prince of Soccer?* (Highdown, 2004)

Malloy, Andy & Danny Malloy, *The Danny Malloy Story: Memoirs of a Hard Man* (Vertical Editions, 2013)

Merrick, Gil, *I See It All* (Museum Press Limited, 1954)

Risoli, Mario, *John Charles: Gentle Giant* (Mainstream Publishing, 2003)

Risoli, Mario, *When Pelé Broke Our Hearts: Wales and the 1958 World Cup* (Ashley Drake Publishing, 1998)

Shindler, Colin, *National Service* (Sphere, 2012)

Ward, Adam & Jeremy Griffen, *The Essential History of Aston Villa* (Headline Book Publishing, 2002)

About the Author

Neil Palmer is a freelance writer who originally hails from Cardiff and now lives in Bristol with his wife and two grown-up children. Neil has written many football books including the popular *Derby Days* series. He has also written books on Cardiff City and Swansea City. *Trevor Ford: The Authorised Biography* is Neil's eighth book to date. When not writing, Neil spends his time running, collecting sports books and listening to vinyl records in the hope of gaining inspiration for his next project.

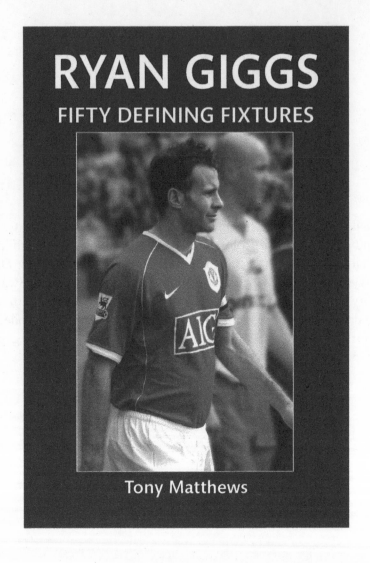